Robert Bernasconi is Moss Professor of Philosophy at the University of Memphis. His books include *The Question of* ___ *e in Heidegger's History of Being and Heidegger in* ___ He has edited anthologies on race and collections of ___ Levinas and Derrida.

THE LON[
www.br

HOW TO READ

Available now

Forthcoming

SARTRE

ROBERT BERNASCONI

Granta Books
London

Granta Publications, 2/3 Hanover Yard, Noel Road, London N1 8BE

First published in Great Britain by Granta Books 2006

CONTENTS

SERIES EDITOR'S FOREWORD

How am I to read *How to Read*?

This series is based on a very simple, but novel idea. Most beginners' guides to great thinkers and writers offer either potted biography or condensed summaries of their major works, or perhaps even both. *How to Read*, by contrast, brings the reader face-to-face with the writing itself in the company of an expert guide. Its starting point is that in order to get close to what a writer is all about, you have to get close to the words they actually use and be shown how to read those words.

Every book in the series is in a way a masterclass in reading. Each author has selected ten or so short extracts from a writer's work and looks at them in detail as a way of revealing their central ideas and thereby opening doors onto a whole world of thought. Sometimes these extracts are arranged chronologically to give a sense of a thinker's development over time, sometimes not. The books are not merely compilations of a thinker's most famous passages, their 'greatest hits', but rather they offer a series of clues or keys that will enable readers to go on and make discoveries of their own. In addition to the texts and readings, each book provides a short biographical chronology and suggestions for further reading, internet resources, and so on. The books in the *How to Read* series don't claim to tell you all you need to know about Freud, Nietzsche and Darwin, or indeed Shakespeare and the Marquis de Sade, but they do offer the best starting point for further exploration.

Unlike the available second-hand versions of the minds that have shaped our intellectual, cultural, religious, political and scientific landscape, *How to Read* offers a refreshing set of first-hand encounters with those minds. Our hope is that these books will, by turn, instruct, intrigue, embolden, encourage and delight.

Simon Critchley
New School for Social Research, New York

ACKNOWLEDGEMENTS

I would like to express my gratitude to the following: Simon Critchley for inviting me to write this volume; Bryan Bannon and Adam Schwartz for reading the manuscript and suggesting changes; George Miller and Bella Shand of Granta Press for being wonderful editors to work with; and Cassandra Dotson for preparing the manuscript without allowing it to diminish her usual good spirits.

INTRODUCTION

When Sartre died in 1980 at the age of seventy-four, more
than fifty thousand people attended his funeral in Paris. This
would have been remarkable at any time, but it happened
when his philosophical works were widely dismissed as *passé*
and when his radical political stances, particularly the encour-
agement he gave to extremist left-wing groups, were
dismissed as irrelevant. In the end Sartre's fame was greater
than the status accorded to both his philosophical and his
political ideas. For at least the first twenty years after the end
of the Second World War, he had been the dominant intellectual figure, not just in France, but in the world. Everyone
everywhere, it seems, had heard of Sartre. His notoriety tran-
scended the political boundaries between the West and the
Soviet bloc, as well as the economic boundaries between
north and south. He wrote novels, plays and newspaper articles in an effort to reach a broader audience, but at the end of
the day his contributions were reduced to one simple image:
Sartre the existentialist, sitting in a café writing weighty philosophical tomes that were judged virtually unreadable.

It has to be admitted that Sartre himself was partly responsible for the difficulty of reading him. He was capable of
writing brilliant prose in spurts, but he rarely maintained this
quality. And he wrote incessantly. It would be all too easy in

a book of this kind to identify ten short captivating extracts
that could be guaranteed to exhilarate their readers, but that
would not take one to the heart of his thinking: at the end of
the volume one would be no closer to having learned how to
read Sartre.

The extracts that follow include some of his most brilliant
pieces of writing. I have put alongside them his presentation
of some of his most difficult ideas. These are worth the effort
necessary to understand them. He did not always write great
prose; he often tortured the French language. Furthermore, to
explain himself, he preferred, especially near the end of his
life, to write more and more, instead of revising and rework-
ing the original formulations until they became clear. It was
not easy to select just five hundred words from *Being and
Nothingness* or *Critique of Dialectical Reason*, two books of well
over five hundred pages. Sartre was never inclined to try to say
anything significant in five hundred words, if he could string
it out. That is why the selection of the extracts has not been
possible without the use of ellipses.

Sartre is not merely difficult; he courts misunderstanding.
He seems almost incapable of issuing a measured statement
when an exaggeration might be more provocative. He writes
to get the reader's attention rather than to solicit their agreement. Unfortunately this tendency is as present in the interviews,
when he dismisses some of his early works as absurd, as it is in
those early works themselves. This makes him an easy target for
his critics.

Nevertheless, any balanced overview of Sartre cannot help
but be overwhelmed by his extraordinary achievements. Even
if some of his literary works are excessively didactic, his early
collection of short stories *The Wall* and the novel *Nausea*,
both of which were published in the 1930s, are masterpieces.

His early philosophical treatises on the emotions, the ego and the imagination have proved to be of lasting interest. He may justly be criticized for making *Being and Nothingness* unnecessarily difficult to read, but it is nevertheless one of the few works of so-called continental philosophy that has consistently attracted the attention of analytical philosophers not known for their tolerance of jargon. Similarly, a number of essays from the late 1940s that were written simply as occasional pieces, like *Anti-Semite and Jew*, 'Black Orpheus' and 'Existentialism is a Humanism', have attained the status of classics. In 1947, in *What is Literature?*, Sartre developed the idea of the committed or engaged writer, and from that point on his commitment to change the world was never in doubt. He spent much of the 1950s re-educating himself so that at the end of the decade he was able to present in *Critique of Dialectical Reason* a Marxism reinvigorated by existentialism.

Sartre wrote from a sense of urgency and, for example when engaging the political issues of the day, such as torture, decolonization, the Vietnam War, and the student revolution of May 1968, he would sacrifice his health for his work. Nevertheless, even at the end of his life he did not let up. Although some of his political allies criticized him for addressing such a 'bourgeois' theme, he persisted with his long-standing project to write an existential biography of Gustave Flaubert under the title *The Idiot of the Family*, producing three massive volumes in the early 1970s. In short, he embodied his idea of the committed intellectual by successfully combining the lives of a novelist, a playwright, a philosopher, an editor and a political activist.

Sartre is still studied today in academic circles, but even though his name is familiar to everyone, he is not read as much as he should be by the broader public. In part this is because his texts often make uncomfortable reading: one goes to Sartre expecting to be indulged in one's existential crisis and finds oneself being told instead to take responsibility for the whole world. The popular image of Sartrean existentialism is of self-absorption, but one soon discovers that he leads one directly to politics. Sartre's philosophy calls for commitment: not in the sense of promises that bind one's future, but in the sense of involvement, working for others politically.

However, the politics Sartre espoused are even less popular now than they were in his own time. In the so-called First World of affluent nations he is often presented as an apologist for oppressive regimes. There is some truth to this: he made numerous serious errors of political judgement. Nevertheless, many of these issues seem a great deal clearer in retrospect than they did at the time. It is not always easy for new readers to understand how different the world looked in the years immediately after the Second World War. It was not only the United States and Britain that had rescued France, but the Soviet Union also, and the Soviet Union was at that time a great deal more vociferous about its ideals than the United States, which was unapologetic in its championing of racial apartheid. It is not without basis that John Gerassi subtitled his biography of Sartre 'Hated Conscience of His Century'.

Sartre is seen very differently in the Third World and he is still read there as the champion of the oppressed. He not only took up their cause but did everything in his power to let them be heard. The pages of *Les Temps Modernes*, the monthly journal he co-founded after the Second World War with a group of like-minded Parisian intellectuals, was open to the spokesmen and -women of the Third World, and

Sartre used his reputation to gain them an audience. Some of the introductions he contributed to their books are still read today for their intrinsic interest. To be sure, his eagerness to give a hearing to these authors, famous now but neglected at the time, had the inevitable result that some of the positions he adopted now seem dated and open to criticism. One sees this, for example, in relation to 'Black Orpheus', his introduction to an anthology of poems associated with the negritude movement. That was in 1948 and already within a couple of years Frantz Fanon was complaining about it, even while acknowledging his continuing admiration for Sartre. It was in the same spirit that, late in his life, Sartre risked arrest by distributing Maoist newspapers, not because he agreed with them but because he thought they deserved a hearing.

Nevertheless, one should not idolize him. It is hard to explain, let alone justify, his failure to lend the full weight of his support to feminism. It is astonishing that he could have lived most of his life with Simone de Beauvoir, author of *The Second Sex*, and not become more sensitive to this issue that represents one of the most decisive global movements of his time.

Sartre wrote at a time when mainstream philosophy seemed to have completely lost touch with the kind of questions about our responsibilities and about the meaning of life that ordinary people expect it to address. Sartre more than anybody kept those ancient questions alive and that is why, even among those who did not like his answers, he came to be *the* philosopher of his generation. Sartre was not an academic's philosopher so much as a regular person's philosopher: indeed, he stopped teaching philosophy when he was called up to the army before the Second World War and never

returned to it. Existentialism is still one of the most popular
courses that a philosophy department can teach; and now that
it seems as if mainstream philosophy has once again lost touch
with ordinary people, it is again time to read Sartre and learn
from him.

1

'I TOO WAS SUPERFLUOUS'

I was in the municipal park just now. The root of the chestnut tree plunged into the ground just underneath my bench. I no longer remembered that it was a root. Words had disappeared, and with them the meaning of things, the methods of using them, the feeble landmarks which men have traced on their surface. [. . .] And then I had this revelation.

It took my breath away. Never, until these last few days, had I suspected what it meant to 'exist'. [. . .]

We were a heap of existents inconvenienced, embarrassed by ourselves, we hadn't the slightest reason for being there, any of us, each existent, embarrassed, vaguely ill at ease, felt superfluous in relation to the others. *Superfluous*: that was the only connexion I could establish between those trees, those gates, those pebbles. [. . .]

And I – weak, languid, obscene, digesting, tossing about dismal thoughts – I *too was superfluous*. [. . .]

The word Absurdity is now born beneath my pen; a little while ago, in the park, I didn't find it, but then I wasn't looking for it either, I didn't need it: I was thinking without words, *about* things, *with* things. Absurdity was not an idea in my head, or the sound of a voice, but that long dead snake at my feet, that wooden snake. Snake or claw or root or vulture's talon, it doesn't matter. And without formulating anything clearly, I understood that I had found the key to Existence, the key to my Nausea, to my own life. In fact, all that I was able to grasp afterwards comes down to this fundamental absurdity. [. . .]

The essential thing is contingency. I mean that, by definition, existence is not necessity. To exist is simply *to be there*; what exists appears, lets itself be *encountered*, but you can never *deduce* it. There are people, I believe, who have understood that. Only they have tried to overcome this contingency by inventing a necessary, causal being. But no necessary being can explain existence: contingency is not an illusion, an appearance which can be dissipated; it is absolute, and consequently perfect gratuitousness. Everything is gratuitous, that park, this town, and myself. [. . .]

The trees [. . .] did not want to exist, only they could not help it; that was the point. [. . .] Tired and old, they went on existing, unwillingly and ungraciously, simply because they were too weak to die, because death could come to them only from the outside: melodies alone can proudly carry their own death within them like an internal necessity; only they don't exist. Every existent is born without reason, prolongs itself out of weakness and dies by chance. I leaned back and I closed my eyes. But pictures, promptly informed, sprang forward and filled my closed eyes with existences: existence is a repletion which man can never abandon.

Nausea.

Although Sartre did not publish *Nausea* until the spring of 1938, he had already completed a draft in 1934. Initially the book was to have been called *Melancholia*, after Albrecht Dürer's engraving, but at the suggestion of the publisher it was given the title that in retrospect seems the only one possible. The novel consists of a series of diary entries by Antoine Roquentin, a solitary thirty-year-old who, after a period of travelling, settles in the town of Bouville so as to write a biography of the Marquis de Rollebon. Roquentin keeps the diary to record a transformation that he is undergoing: 'I must say how I see this table, the street, people, my packet of tobacco, since *these* are the things which have changed.' In other words, Sartre has Roquentin do precisely what Sartre himself turned to phenomenology to help him do: to offer a description of things. The difference is that here the description is of how things look when one suffers from nausea. Nausea makes disappear the familiar aspect of things that allows us to recognize them. The residue that remains is what Sartre calls here 'existence'. We know from Simone de Beauvoir's *The Prime of Life* that Sartre's manuscript began as a discussion of contingency, and it was at her suggestion that he introduced the fictional depth that has secured the work its long-standing popularity. However, even though *Nausea* is a highly philosophical book, it is a mistake to try to read into it Sartre's later philosophy, although this is often done. It must be read on its own terms.

The scene in the park, from which the above extract is drawn, is widely recognized as the central scene of the novel. However, it should also be noted that, taken in isolation, the passage is somewhat misleading. For one thing, it focuses largely on Roquentin's relation to things, to the exclusion of his relation with other human beings. It is necessary, therefore, to establish some context for reading it.

Roquentin finds that he cannot justify his existence. His

problem is not with the quality of his life. Nor does he ask whether life is worth living or not, as if he was facing a decision about whether or not to continue to exist. His point is simply that there is no reason to exist at all. His discovery of this begins when he stares at a small statuette while he is still in Indo-China and asks himself why he is there. At a loss for a reason, he returns to France, but, unlike the other customers of the cafés he frequents, who find solace in the company of others, he for some time justifies his existence in terms of his project to write a biography of Rollebon. However, Rollebon begins to bore him, and before long the project loses its appeal for him. He thereby discovers that the tasks one sets oneself only serve to veil what, in the passage under consideration, he comes to call the absurdity of existence. Visiting the portraits of the town's leading citizens at the museum, he feels as though these men who did not question their lives and privileges were calling into question his own right to exist. It is after he finds that he cannot proceed with writing the biography that he undergoes the experience in the park in which he receives his revelation of the meaning of existence.

Roquentin discovers that, to the extent that things lose their functionality, it is no longer possible to see their existence as natural. When they are robbed of the role to which he assigns them, the categories by which he organizes them, the relationships in which he situates them, and the words with which he names them, they lose their individuality; there is no apparent reason why they exist. However, the loss of language that deprives things of their significance, in the sense of their place in the world, makes the fact of their existence even more pronounced. Roquentin had previously equated existence with the present and supposed that behind things there is nothing. Now it seems that existence itself is nothing; it is simply an empty form that changes nothing. As Kant wrote: 'being is not a real predicate'. However, what Roquentin discovers is that things are 'too much'. The French phrase he uses is *de trop*, and its meaning is somewhat indeterminate. Roquentin means that things are excessive; they are superfluous. In *Being and Nothingness* Sartre conceded that the expression 'being is superfluous (*de trop*)' is anthropomorphic. The proper philosophical way of highlighting the contingency of being is simply to say: being-in-itself is. The contingency of being consists in the fact that one cannot derive one thing from another; they are not in a necessary relation with each other. But it is not only things that are superfluous; Roquentin himself is superfluous. Just as the existence of 'things' comes to the fore when they appear to lose their utility, so Roquentin's existence comes to the fore when he can no longer locate the purpose of his existence in writing a book about Rollebon.

What then is nausea for Sartre? He gives more than one description, so it is not easy to generalize, but it seems that the differences between the descriptions are not inconsistencies but are supposed to reflect Roquentin's education in nausea. Their impact on the reader is similarly cumulative. Certain features are clear. The nausea seizes Roquentin: he has no control over it; it comes from outside and overwhelms him. Indeed, Sartre emphasizes that the nausea is 'out there' (*là-bas*) and that he is inside of it, in keeping with his account of intentionality. Roquentin gives greater determinacy to his experience of nausea when he introduces the idea that absurdity is the key to both his existence and the nausea that reveals it. That is to say, he discovers that it is not through thought that he gains access to existence as such, but in

nausea. Through nausea he discovers the absurdity of existence: he cannot say why what exists does exist rather than
not exist. This does not lead him to commit suicide, because
even in death one remains superfluous. The claim that existence cannot be deduced, that it is not necessary but
contingent, highlights the way in which Sartre is already pre-
senting an account that would interfere with attempts to
prove the existence of God. This is a fundamentally atheistic
philosophy.

The sentence near the end of the extract that contrasts the
death of trees and the death of melodies evokes a theme that
Sartre returns to throughout the book and is clearly central to
its meaning, although from the time of its first publication
readers have not agreed on what that meaning is. Roquentin
repeatedly requests that the café play a certain jazz record,
'Some of These Days'. In contrast with the contingency of
existence that for Roquentin characterizes things and even
himself, the music displays a certain necessity and in so doing
cures his nausea. Hence, Roquentin wonders if he could not
give his own life the character of a melody. More specifically,
he wonders if the answer to his problem does not lie in having
an adventure, because, unlike life in general, adventures share
with melodies the characteristic of having a beginning and an
end. However, he discovers that this is not so easy and that
there is an artificiality to the construction of an adventure.
Nevertheless, even if Sartre rejects taking an aesthetic attitude
to life here, as in the conclusion of *The Imaginary*, the possibility remains that one can become an artist − like the black
woman who sings the song or the Jew who Roquentin imag-
ines wrote it − by writing, not a history book about reality,
but a work of fiction about what could never happen, an
adventure.

We know that later in life Sartre would reject the idea that art brings salvation, but what was his position in 1938? The historical evidence suggests that at the time he probably still believed in salvation through literature, at least for himself, but that does not mean that that was the point the novel was supposed to convey. The salvation Roquentin anticipates is that people might be able to recall his life without repugnance, precisely because he had created a work of art that would make him legendary, like the singer and the songwriter. However, Roquentin had already conceded that neither the singer nor the songwriter would have thought about themselves as he thought about them. Is it enough for Roquentin that others think of him as legendary? It seems not. It seems that this solitary man wants to be able to recall his own life without repugnance. He surmises that, if he were successful, he would be able to say that his salvation began when he made this resolution to write his novel. It is unlikely that Sartre did not recognize the problem: Roquentin has simply reverted to thinking of his life as an adventure with a real beginning. He has once again failed to respect the difference between a life, which exists, and a work of art, which, according to Sartre, does not. Although some commentators see Sartre as opting for an aestheticist solution outside life or reality, this solution does not seem to make sense in terms of the frame of reference of the novel. As Sartre confirms in the *War Diaries* in February 1940, being part of an adventure is 'an unrealizable' in the sense that it appears only in retrospect in the account one gives of it. Sartre tries to show why the desire to be at the centre of some beautiful event, to be the author of a painting or song, is so powerful, but also why this way of negotiating existence necessarily fails.

The final phrase of the extract reads: 'existence is a repletion which man can never abandon'. It is not an easy sentence
to understand, but fortunately Sartre returns to it in *The War
Diaries* in the context of his reading of Heidegger's *Being and
Time*. In an entry from December 1939 he takes over explicitly from Heidegger the idea that a human being exists in the
future, in the sense that it relates to itself in terms of the possibilities that it projects for itself. Sartre understands this to
mean that human reality is limited by the aim it sets itself. In
this context he returns to the claim he made in *Nausea* about
the fullness of existence and comments that although he
would not retract that claim, he would now add that this fullness is human. In other words, the human being discovers his
or her project everywhere and discovers only this project.
One might ask whether this does not mean that, at least in
one respect, Sartre has reverted to the digestive philosophy
that he had sought to overcome in 'Intentionality': everywhere
we encounter only ourselves. He subsequently, as we shall see,
adopted and enriched Heidegger's notion of facticity, understood as the 'that it is' of human existence, to correct that
impression. However, what is important here is that in *The
War Diaries* Sartre acknowledges that Heidegger helped him
to see that the connection between human beings and
things was even closer than he had recognized in *Nausea*, or
in the brief essay 'Intentionality' (to which we shall turn
next). It is by freely projecting the possibilities of one's existence that one determines how one sees things, what
function they have, and their place in the world. That is
why the breakdown of one's project, such as Roquentin
suffers when he loses interest in writing a historical biography, not only deprives a person of meaning but also leads
things to lose their significance. Under these conditions it

becomes impossible for Roquentin to integrate things into his world. In his subsequent philosophical works Sartre sought new ways to explore the intimate relation of human beings and things.

'OUTSIDE, IN THE WORLD, AMONG OTHERS'

Sartre's short essay 'Intentionality' was one of his first attempts to write original philosophy: he wrote it in 1934 while he was studying in Germany, but waited five years to publish it. It expresses with characteristic directness the enthusiasm he felt on learning about phenomenology (literally the study of appearances), the philosophical school with which he identified in all of his philosophical publications for the next ten years, and from which he never fully departed.

In 'Intentionality' Sartre conveys with impressive directness his enthusiasm for the idea that philosophy might be put back in touch with concrete experience by being released from the sterile epistemological debates that had preoccupied it for most of the last three hundred years. The foremost of these debates was that between realism and idealism. Conventionally, realism maintains that material things exist independently of our minds, whereas idealism, in its dominant sense, maintains that the only things we know to exist are the non–material ideas in our minds.

'He devoured her with his eyes.' This expression and many other signs point to the illusion common to both realism and

idealism: to know is to eat. After a hundred years of academ-
icism, French philosophy remains at that point. [. . .]
Against the digestive philosophy of empirico-criticism, of neo-
Kantianism, against all 'psychologism,' Husserl persistently
affirmed that one cannot dissolve things in consciousness.
You see this tree, to be sure. But you see it just where it is: at
the side of the road, in the midst of the dust, alone and
writhing in the heat, eight miles from the Mediterranean
coast. It could not enter into your consciousness, for it is not
of the same nature as consciousness. One is perhaps
reminded of Bergson and the first chapter of *Matter and
Memory*. But Husserl is not a realist: this tree on its bit of
parched earth is not an absolute which would subsequently
enter into communication with us. Consciousness and the
world are given at one stroke: essentially external to consciousness, the world is nevertheless essentially relative to
consciousness. Husserl sees consciousness as an irreducible
fact which no physical image can account for. Except perhaps
the quick, obscure image of a burst. To know is to 'burst
toward,' to tear oneself out of the moist gastric intimacy, veer-
ing out there beyond oneself, out there near the tree and yet
beyond it, for the tree escapes me and repulses me, and I can
no more lose myself in the tree than it can dissolve itself in
me. I'm beyond it; it's beyond me.

Do you recognize in this description your own circumstances and your own impressions? You certainly knew that
the tree was not you, that you could not make it enter your
dark stomach and that knowledge could not, without dishon-
esty, be compared to possession. [. . .]
Being, says Heidegger, is being-in-the-world. One must understand this 'being-in' as movement. To be is to fly out into the
world, to spring from the nothingness of the world and of

consciousness in order suddenly to burst out as conscious-ness-in-the-world. When consciousness tries to recoup itself, to coincide with itself once and for all, closeted off all warm and cosy, it destroys itself. This necessity for consciousness to exist as consciousness of something other than itself Husserl calls 'intentionality'. [. . .]

He has cleared the way for a new treatise on the passions which would be inspired by this simple truth, so utterly ignored by the refined among us: if we love a woman, it is because she is lovable. We are delivered from Proust. We are likewise delivered from the 'internal life'.

[. . .] everything is finally outside, everything, even ourselves. Outside, in the world, among others. It is not in some hiding-place that we will discover ourselves; it is on the road, in the town, in the midst of the crowd, a thing among things, a man among men.

'Intentionality: A Fundamental Idea of Husserl's Phenomenology.'

Phenomenology was introduced by Edmund Husserl (1859–1938) in 1900 in an effort to return philosophy to 'the things themselves' and to do so in a way that was rigorously scientific. Sartre was less attracted to the scientific preten-sions of phenomenology than to the idea that it would provide him with the means to describe concrete objects, and to do so as a philosopher. As soon as he learned about Husserlian phenomenology in 1933, he arranged to go to the French Institute in Berlin to learn more about it. During the year he spent there, he wrote the essay on intentionality, 'Transcendence of the Ego', a powerful essay drawing out the philosophical implications of the idea of intentionality for an understanding of the self, as well as an early draft of his novel *Nausea*. However, as Simone de Beauvoir (1908–86) tells us in *The Prime of Life*, even in the midst of Sartre's initial excitement at discovering phenomenology, he immediately expressed anxiety about how this impacted on his sense of his own originality. He need not have worried. Even though he presented his essay on intentionality in the form of an exposition, it is no surprise to find that Husserl scholars do not regard it as providing a faithful representation of Husserl's position.

When Sartre discovered Husserl, he was already disillusioned with what he regarded as tired academic debates between rival positions, all of which seemed to place human beings at an artificial distance from the world. For him there was no clearer indication of this than the way philosophers, in their quest for certainty, had come to focus on the contents of consciousness. The conventional view was that we can legitimately claim to know the ideas in our heads, but this leaves unresolved the question of how we know that these contents of consciousness correspond to things in the world. In other words, the study of philosophy had come to be dominated by epistemological questions, questions of knowledge. However, philosophers had set the problem up in such a way as to make it virtually insoluble. Sartre saw that it was necessary to focus once more on our concrete dealings with things and that the only way that that could be done was by transforming the philosophical take on how human beings relate to things in the world.

The appeal of Husserl's conception of intentionality to Sartre was that it enabled philosophers to do precisely that. Husserl, like the Austrian philosopher Franz Brentano (1838–1917), from whom he borrowed the idea, defined intentionality in terms of the formula 'consciousness is consciousness of something'. That is to say, consciousness is not thing-like, but a directionality towards things. By isolating Husserl's idea of intentionality from other more technical elements of his philosophy, Sartre sought to free it in order to fulfil Husserl's own aim of getting back to the things themselves.

One of the most technical components and one that Sartre regarded as especially responsible for Husserl's failure, in his eyes, to arrive at the things themselves was the so-called phenomenological reduction. This was a procedure whereby the philosopher suspends belief in the existence of the world and thereby passes from the naivety of everyday life and enters a realm of certainty of the kind that, according to Husserl, the philosopher seeks. By refusing the phenomenological reduction, Sartre, according to orthodox Husserlians, remained locked in the naivety of concrete existence. So as far as they are concerned, he is not doing phenomenology. In fact Sartre, as we saw in the previous selection, had his own form of the reduction, but it was not a technique but an event that is open to description. Indeed, Sartre identifies the force of phenomenology with the power to persuade readers to recognize their own experience through descriptions. Hence Sartre's question to his readers: 'Do you recognize in this description your own circumstances and your own impressions?' For Sartre, the method of description legitimizes not just the concept of intentionality, but all of his philosophy.

Sartre employs descriptions in an attempt to bypass philosophical debates, like that between realism and idealism, but at the end of the day he is left, like any other philosopher, articulating a position, so that, in reading his philosophical works, one is always left asking whether the descriptions do indeed support the positions taken rather than undermine them. If one examines how in the essay 'Intentionality' Sartre negotiates the realism-idealism debate, one finds already in the first couple of paragraphs a certain incoherence in the way his presentation of the idea of intentionality relates to the philosophical debate that he sketches there. The opening lines of the essay make it apparent that part of the fundamental attraction of the idea of intentionality to Sartre is that it takes us beyond the gesture of assimilating things to consciousness that is common to both realism and idealism. Hence he labels them both as 'digestive' philosophies, the more readily to leave both behind in a single step. However, when in the next paragraph he introduces Husserl as the foremost proponent of this idea of intentionality, he is able to say only that Husserl was not a realist. If intentionality in and of itself secured a passage beyond both realism and idealism, then one might think that Husserl would not be an idealist either. The problem was that in 1913 in *Ideas Pertaining to a Pure Phenomenology*, Husserl had embraced idealism, to the disappointment of some of his followers, including most importantly the young Martin Heidegger (1889–1976), who continued to prefer the early Husserl of the *Logical Investigations*. The contrast Sartre draws at the beginning of the essay on intentionality between Husserl and Henri Bergson (1859–1941), who was at the time the most prestigious French philosopher alive, is therefore somewhat disingenuous. What is left unstated is that in 1896 in *Matter and Memory* Bergson, seeking to overcome the dualism of his earlier work, had already sought to show what realism and idealism had in common, the better to leave both behind. It is therefore in terms of Bergson's philosophical ambition to leave this particular debate behind that Sartre proposes to approach intentionality. If it is possible for Sartre to imply that Bergson can be read as some kind of realist, then in the context of the argument, Husserl's explicit idealism should also have been brought into consideration and not left unstated as it was by Sartre, particularly as we know that at this time he was preoccupied with Husserl's *Ideas* at the expense of the *Logical Investigations*. To be sure, by keeping silent about Husserl's idealism, Sartre was not attempting to conceal anything: he was merely postponing a direct confrontation with the various ways in which he believed Husserl had compromised his own original insight into intentionality, most especially by holding fast to the ego, instead of seeing it as a product of reflection. In any event, Sartre was not alone in attempting to draw on the idea of intentionality as part of an effort to surpass the debate between realism and idealism: Heidegger had announced similar ambitions in *Being and Time* in 1927.

Sartre would not study Heidegger's *Being and Time* with any care until the Second World War. Once he did, his thinking would undergo a decisive transformation. However, to see that, one needs to be clear about how Sartre's initial response to Husserl's conception of intentionality differed from that of Heidegger. I shall focus on three points of contrast.

First, Heidegger offered an account of human existence that explicitly sought to overcome the primacy accorded to epistemology (or the theory of knowledge) over ontology (the theory of being). His complaint was that neglect of ontology, and more precisely a growing tendency among philosophers to fail to highlight the difference between the way human beings exist and the kind of being things have, led modern philosophy to focus on the problem of knowledge. For example, whereas Immanuel Kant (1724–1804) had called it a scandal that there was no proof for the existence of the external world, Heidegger's response was that the world was not external, that the human being understood as being-there

(*Dasein*) belonged in the world by the very nature of its existence, and that the real scandal was that such a proof had
been sought at all. It was because Heidegger no longer
thought of the world as external and thus distinct from human
beings, but as in a very precise sense integral to human existence, that he understood the human being as a
'being-in-the-world'. Although Sartre already adopts this formulation in the essay on intentionality, we shall see later that
he did not fully see its implications until much later. At this
time, that is to say, in the 1930s, Sartre was less violently
opposed to the primacy of epistemology in modern philosophy than Heidegger. The possibility highlighted by
phenomenology, of analysing the different ways in which a
consciousness relates to its objects – depending, for example,
on whether it simply sought to know them or whether there
was some emotional involvement – led Sartre to look to various philosophical investigations outside of epistemology. So,
for example, over the next few years he proceeded to write a
draft of a new treatise on the passions under the title *The
Psyche*. The main trace of this endeavour in 'Intentionality'
was his attempt to extend the analysis of consciousness as
consciousness of something to acts like love and hate: 'if we
love a woman, it is because she is lovable'. The wonderfully
simple idea that if I love someone it is because that person is
lovable delivers the discourse of love from obsessive introspection, and places its focus back firmly where it belongs: on
the beloved.

This confirms the depth of Sartre's early opposition to the
philosophy of René Descartes (1596–1650), even if he did not
always find it at all easy to escape from its spell. Particularly
during the Second World War, but also after it, he was in the
habit of evoking Descartes' thought as a precursor of his own

in places where this seemed only to muddy the waters. Later he would excuse himself on the grounds that he wanted to appeal to a French thinker, in an effort to place some distance between him and the German thinkers who were his main inspiration. Whether or not one accepts this – and objections to Sartre's Cartesianism have proved persistent – it took some time for Sartre to learn all the lessons he would eventually glean from Heidegger's attempt to leave the philosophy of Descartes behind. So far as Heidegger was concerned, Husserl was still far too Cartesian in his reliance on the subject–object model as a grid for understanding the relation of human beings with things, and his insistence on epistemological issues. It was to avoid these tendencies, which placed an almost unbridgeable gap between human beings and things, that Heidegger had introduced his idea of human existence as being-in-the-world.

In spite of the fact that both Heidegger and Sartre were committed to the idea that, by reducing the tree to a content of consciousness, philosophy had not yet let the tree stand where it stands out there in the ground, they looked in different directions in order to address the issue. This provides a second point of contrast between them. Sartre was not wrong in 1934 to characterize Heidegger's being-in-the-world as a directional movement towards things, but it only touches the surface of Heidegger's fundamental point. By referring to intentionality as the name of a problem rather than a solution, Heidegger in 'On the Essence of Ground', an essay from 1929, had already sought to open up an entirely new ontological conception of the world as that wherein we dwell, a conception fundamentally distinct from the conventional idea of the world as the sum total of all the things in it. Sartre at this time and for some considerable time to come failed to break free from this prevailing conception of the world and so remained deaf to what Heidegger had already begun to call 'the clearing' (*Lichtung*). Heidegger's clearing borrows from the idea of a forest clearing as the open space that first allows the trees and other inhabitants of the forest to be seen. Heidegger regarded the clearing as indispensable to his attempt to think of the primacy of the *relation* of human existence to things over the things related. Sartre's effort to think intentionality more deeply was, by contrast, always marked by a certain impatience to arrive at the concrete, and all ontological considerations were subordinated to that.

This marks a third decisive difference: Sartre's retention of the word 'consciousness'. Because Heidegger discarded the term, French Heideggerians saw Sartre's continuing employment of it as evidence of his failure to abandon Descartes' starting point in the human subject. To a certain extent, the charge is unfair. Sartre's critical examination of the evidence supplied by reflection rendered the term all but indispensable. In 'Transcendence of the Ego', Sartre argues that when one turns inward to examine one's own states one creates a new object, the ego, that had previously not existed. For Sartre, there is no independent subject of the classical kind, access to which is secured, as Descartes believed, by introspection, an inspection of the mind. Consciousness cannot know itself independent of its relation to things. Far from being a privileged form of self-knowledge, introspection is for Sartre largely deceptive. Hence, the essay on intentionality closes by separating the procedure of phenomenological description from the technique of introspection exemplified by the novels of Marcel Proust (1871–1922).

But what is Sartre able to say here positively about consciousness, beyond introducing the image of a bursting or explosion (*éclatement*) or a flight of consciousness in an effort to explain this movement to which it is reduced? His subsequent philosophical writings, especially *Being and Nothingness*, attempt to formulate the ontology that would allow us to sustain these descriptions as philosophy. In the process, the descriptions themselves, and not just their terms, undergo some modification. In 'Intentionality', Sartre describes – in the context of his account of Heidegger, but it seems he underwrites it – how, for a human being, to exist is 'to spring from the nothingness of the world and of consciousness in order suddenly to burst out as consciousness-in-the-world'. This is another way of saying that neither consciousness, nor 'the thing', has priority and that we have no way of describing either of them prior to the moment of their encounter.

However, in *Being and Nothingness* the term 'nothingness', which in 'Intentionality' is used to describe both consciousness and thing, is reserved for consciousness alone. This nothingness of consciousness is not a passive non-existence, but an escape from the current world towards the future world into which consciousness projects itself. Hence this nothingness of consciousness is said by Sartre to lie 'coiled at the heart of being – like a worm'. In so far as this is a departure from what is said in 'Intentionality,' and not merely a modification imposed by the attempt to translate the description into an ontology, this is because *Being and Nothingness* reflects, in this respect as in others, the growing impact of Heidegger's thought on Sartre, an impact that continues to be felt in the late works. Nevertheless, in *Being and Nothingness* Sartre sets out from the distinction between the for-itself of consciousness and the in-itself of being in the sense of the thing. Heidegger would never have accepted this dualistic ontology as a starting point, but one can at least grant that Sartre never intended this to be his last word. From the outset he insisted that this division represented an abstraction that was to be overcome through the descriptions. Some of Sartre's most penetrating attempts to do that work are examined in the following chapters.

3

'HELL IS OTHER PEOPLE'

The idea behind *No Exit* is brilliantly simple. Sartre was asked to write a play for three of his friends, including Albert Camus, with the proviso that it should be straightforward to stage, so that they could easily take it on tour. He wanted the actors to be on stage together for the whole of the play so that he did not appear to be favouring one of them over the other. His first idea was to have them trapped in a cellar, seeking shelter from artillery fire. He then had the idea of placing them in hell. Apparently everything else followed smoothly. He wrote the play in two weeks in late 1943, and it was first performed early the following summer while Paris was still occupied by the Germans. At one point the German censor threatened to withhold permission to perform the play, but subsequently relented. (Ironically, in 1946 the Lord Chancellor did ban the play, because it depicts a lesbian. The curious result is that it was accepted by the Nazi authorities, but could not be staged in Britain.)

GARCIN: Listen! Each man has an aim in life, a leading motive; that's so, isn't it? Well, I didn't give a damn for wealth, or for love. I aimed at being a real man. A tough, as they say. I staked everything on the same horse . . . Can one possibly be a coward when one's deliberately courted danger at every turn? And can one judge a life by a single action?

INEZ: Why not? For thirty years you dreamt you were a hero, and condoned a thousand petty lapses – because a hero, of course, can do no wrong. An easy method, obviously. Then a day came when you were up against it, the red light of real danger – and you took the train to Mexico.

GARCIN: I 'dreamt,' you say. It was no dream. When I chose the hardest path, I made my choice deliberately. A man is what he wills himself to be.

INEZ: Prove it. Prove it was no dream. It's what one does, and nothing else, that shows the stuff one's made of.

GARCIN: I died too soon. I wasn't allowed time to – to do my deeds.

INEZ: One always dies too soon – or too late. And yet one's whole life is complete at that moment, with a line drawn neatly under it, ready for the summing up. You are – your life, and nothing else.

GARCIN: What a poisonous woman you are! With an answer for everything.

INEZ: [. . .] You're a coward, Garcin, because I wish it. I wish it – do you hear? – I wish it. And yet, just look at me, see how weak I am, a mere breath on the air, a gaze observing you, a formless thought that thinks you. (*He walks towards her, opening his hands*). Ah, they're open now, those big hands, those coarse, man's hands! But what do you hope to do? You can't throttle thoughts with hands. So you've no choice, you must convince me, and you're at my mercy.

ESTELLE: Garcin!

GARCIN: What?

ESTELLE: Revenge yourself.

GARCIN: How?

ESTELLE: Kiss me, darling – then you'll hear her squeal.

GARCIN: That's true, Inez. I'm at your mercy, but you're at mine as well.

(*He bends over* ESTELLE. INEZ *gives a little cry.*) [. . .]

INEZ: Well, what are you waiting for? Do as you're told. What a lovely scene: coward Garcin holding baby-killer Estelle in his manly arms! Make your stakes, everyone. Will coward Garcin kiss the lady, or won't he dare? What's the betting? I'm watching you, everybody's watching, I'm a crowd all by myself. Do you hear the crowd? Do you hear them muttering, Garcin? Mumbling and muttering. 'Coward! Coward! Coward! Coward!' – that's what they're saying . . . It's no use trying to escape, I'll never let you go. What do you hope to get from her silly lips? Forgetfulness? But I shan't forget you, not I! 'It's I you must convince.' So come to me. I'm waiting. Come along, now . . . Look how obedient he is, like a well-trained dog who comes when his mistress calls. You can't hold him, and you never will.

GARCIN: [. . .] So this is hell. I'd never have believed it. You remember all we were told about the torture-chambers, the fire and brimstone, the 'burning marl.' Old wives' tales! There's no need for red-hot pokers. Hell is – other people!

No Exit

Sartre had originally planned to call the play *The Others* (*Les Autres*), and it was under this title that it was first performed. This title refers to the play's most famous line: 'Hell is – other people!' ('*L'enfer, c'est les autres*'). As one of the characters, Inez, recognizes, the room in which they find themselves is hell, not because it is a torture chamber in the conventional sense, but because each one of them tortures the others. More precisely, what tortures them is the fact that they remain isolated even though they are not alone. None of them can manage on their own. Indeed, each of them feels a strong need for one of the others, but is rebuffed because the one they are looking to for company is reaching out to the third one. Whenever it seems that a couple is forming, the third disrupts their efforts. Hence, before being called *No Exit* the play has sometimes been called in English *Vicious Circle*. As another of the characters, Garcin, says, 'We're chasing after each other, round and round in a vicious circle, like the horses on a roundabout.'

The conflictual character of relations within the play is best illustrated by examining the attractions between them and the rebuffs they subsequently suffer. Garcin, like many of the characters of Sartre's plays and novels, is pretending to be something he is not as a result of his fundamental cowardice. This is particularly graphic in his case because he is a man who, having lived his life under the conviction that he was a hero, shows himself at the decisive moment to be a coward, a deserter. All those who depend on others for validation are hostage to the judgements that those others pass on them. What disturbs Garcin is less the facts, which he can manipulate to his own satisfaction, than the image that the other characters have of him, which he is less able to control. He is so dependent on Estelle's opinion that he even refuses to try to leave the room when the door is left open. Nevertheless, things are not quite so simple. Garcin is right to complain that his whole life should not be reduced to the single action of desertion. On Sartrean grounds, he can no more be a hero than he can *be* a coward, at least in the way a table *is* a table.

Estelle is as much of a coward as Garcin, but unlike Garcin, who refused to kill, she is a murderess. She cheated on her husband and then drowned the baby she had with her lover, who as a result commited suicide. Like Garcin, she is heavily dependent on others for approval. If Garcin wants to be thought of by Estelle as a hero, she in turn wants Garcin to think of her as a respectable woman. However, their complicity in deception is doomed to failure by Inez, who frustrates their efforts by judging them with her eyes. At one point, Estelle even wonders aloud whether she really exists when she cannot see herself in the mirror, and so comes to rely all the more heavily on the mirroring gaze of others.

Inez is a lesbian who makes other people suffer, as she herself readily admits. She responds to the fact that others see her as cruel by being precisely that. She acts out their expectations of her. It was because of her that her lover committed suicide by turning on the gas stove one night, incidentally killing Inez in the process. Inez is the first of all the characters to recognize that their hell consists in the fact that the three are torturing each other. This is perhaps because she knew more suffering in her life than the other characters. She not only suffers herself, but also tortures her lover mentally. Each of the characters is thus dependent on the others. Each hopes, needs, to convince the others that he or she is what he or she wants to be, and so to have that image of him- or herself confirmed.

Garcin is the one who says that 'Hell is — other people!' This leaves the question as to whether Sartre would underwrite the claim himself, as some critics have suggested. The tendency to attribute to Sartre himself the sentiment 'hell is other people' arises in large measure because of the account of human relations presented in *Being and Nothingness*, according to which, in any pairing, each person vies to reduce the other to an object so as to maintain him- or herself in the subject position. The account culminates in an attack on Heidegger's description of human relations in terms of what he calls 'being-with' (*Mitsein*), an expression that, as Sartre says, makes it sound as if we are all on the same team. Sartre concludes: 'The essence of the relations between consciousnesses is not *Mitsein*; it is conflict.'[1] Nevertheless, fifteen years after writing *No Exit* Sartre explicitly denies that he was saying something similar in the play. Explaining that 'hell is other people' had always been misunderstood, in so far as people believed that he meant our relations with others were always poisoned, he insisted that he meant only that, because nothing is more important than others for our understanding of ourselves, then, if our relations with others are warped or depraved, then hell is others. In other words, if hell is other people for us, then *we* are to blame and it could always be otherwise. Whether or not one accepts this explanation, there is at least some confirmation in the fact that each of the characters, when alive, tortured other people: Garcin abused his wife, who was from a lower class than he was, by parading his lovers in front of her; Estelle killed the child her lover wanted; Inez tortured her lover Florence by making her feel responsible for her husband's death.

At the same time that Sartre offered his gloss on the statement that 'hell is other people', he explained that relations with others was only one theme of the play. In this context, he also singled out 'encrustation' and freedom as other themes worthy of attention. Encrustation refers to the difficulty of changing ourselves since others through their gaze transmit an image of us that constrains us and so restricts our freedom. Sartre can be taken as saying that if one lives in the world as if everything is unchangeable, then one has created a hell. To that extent, it would be another way of reminding us that we have adopted an idea of human nature that effectively imprisons us by persuading us that change is impossible. This at least would be in keeping with Sartre's idea of the theatre as a way to show human beings that they are capable of changing the world.

This moral is underlined by the closing line of the play, when Garcin says: 'Well, well, let's get on with it . . .' With this instruction ringing in their ears, the audience are intended to see life differently from the play's characters. The audience, unlike the three characters, can still change their lives. Sartre seems to be suggesting that, like Garcin, Estelle and Inez, they are also trapped, encrusted, but only so long as they maintain the pretence that they are not free. That is to say, the audience is not supposed to identify with the characters in the play. To do so would be to believe that one cannot change, and thus create a hell on earth. The task is to see oneself in a way that the characters cannot see themselves. In any event, 'hell is other people' was not Sartre's final word on the possibility of genuine human relations.

4

'HE IS PLAYING AT BEING A WAITER IN A CAFÉ'

Sartre did not begin to write *Being and Nothingness* until late 1941 and it is remarkable that it had already been published by the summer of 1943, particularly when one considers its length: some 725 pages. Legend has it that it was used as a kilo weight in grocery stores. The speed with which he completed the book accounts for only some of its difficulty. This was for the most part an abstract work of ontology that aimed at concrete existence but never quite seemed to reach it, except in the brilliant phenomenological descriptions which are among the most memorable philosophical examples ever written. To be sure, it is not always clear what they were examples of, but Sartre's description of the ways in which waiters tend to exaggerate their every gesture is one of the most celebrated descriptions in the history of philosophy.

If man is what he is, bad faith is for ever impossible and candour ceases to be his ideal and becomes instead his being. But is man what he is? And more generally, how can he *be* what he is when he exists as consciousness of being? If candour or sincerity is a universal value, it is evident that the maxim 'one must be what one is' does not serve solely as a regulating principle for judgements and concepts by which I express what I am. It posits not merely an ideal of knowing but an ideal of *being*; it proposes for us an absolute equivalence of being with itself as a prototype of being. In this sense it is necessary that we *make ourselves* what we are. But what *are we* then if we have the constant obligation to make ourselves what we are, if our mode of being is having the obligation to be what we are?

Let us consider this waiter in the café. His movement is quick and forward, a little too precise, a little too rapid. He comes toward the patrons with a step a little too quick. He bends forward a little too eagerly; his voice, his eyes express an interest a little too solicitous for the order of the customer. Finally there he returns, trying to imitate in his walk the inflexible stiffness of some kind of automaton while carrying his tray with the recklessness of a tight-rope-walker by putting it in a perpetually unstable, perpetually broken equilibrium which he perpetually re-establishes by a light movement of the arm and hand. All his behaviour seems to us a game. [. . .] He is playing at *being* a waiter in a café. [. . .] the waiter in the café plays with his condition in order to *realize* it. [. . .]

In a parallel situation, from within, the waiter in the café can not be immediately a café waiter in the sense that this inkwell *is* an inkwell [. . .] In vain do I fulfil the functions of a café waiter. I can be he only in the neutralized mode, as the actor is Hamlet, by mechanically making the *typical gestures* of my state and by aiming at myself as an imaginary café waiter through those gestures taken as an 'analogue'.[1] What I attempt to realize is a being-in-itself of the café waiter, as if [. . .] from the very fact that I sustain this role in existence I did not transcend it on every side, as if I did not constitute myself as one *beyond* my condition. Yet there is no doubt that I *am* in a sense a café waiter – otherwise could I not just as well call myself a diplomat or a reporter? But if I am one, this can not be in the mode of being in-itself. I am a waiter in the mode of *being what I am not*.

Being and Nothingness.

It is well known that the above description is presented as an example of bad faith (*mauvaise foi*), that bad faith means something like self-deception, and that Sartre believes that it is pervasive. Nevertheless, one needs to be clearer as to precisely what the example is intended to show.

Sartre's central point with the example of the waiter is to show that consciousness is never simply what it is. A thing can be only what it is, but, however strange it might sound, that is not true of consciousness: nobody is, for example, simply a waiter and nothing else. So, whereas Sartre calls the thing 'being in itself' or, more simply, 'the in-itself', he calls consciousness 'the for-itself' because it is conscious of itself, in the sense of being aware of itself, even without making itself directly its own object. Its self-awareness opens up a fissure or break at the heart of consciousness so that it never simply coincides with itself but, in the form of negation, succeeds always in escaping itself. This capacity for self-negation is crucial to Sartre, who had earlier shown how the self can be negated from outside by another consciousness: the boss in the relation to the worker, the guard in relation to the prisoner, the overseer in relation to the slave, are all negations. The immediate purpose of the discussion of bad faith is to show that consciousness can negate itself.

To show this through the example of the waiter, Sartre cannot be content to show the waiter playing at being a waiter by following certain rules, although this is what most readers seem to notice first. Sartre, in his example, highlights the characteristics of the French waiter, who plays at being a waiter by acting like an automaton, just as the role of a waiter in the United States, by a strange inversion, is to play at acting like one's friend. However, Sartre's point is that, whatever game the waiter is called upon to play, the ultimate rule that the waiter follows is that he must break the rules, and to do so by following them in an exaggerated manner. That is to say, the waiter does not simply follow the unwritten rules, which would be obedience to a certain kind of tyranny, but, instead, goes overboard in following those rules. The waiter succeeds in rejecting the attempt to reduce him to nothing more than being a waiter, not by refusing the role, but by highlighting the fact that he is playing it to the point that he escapes it. The waiter does this by overdoing things, by doing too much. The French waiter, instead of disappearing into the role, exaggerates the movements that make him something of an automaton in a way that draws attention to him, just as, we can add, the quintessential North American waiter is not so much friendly as overfriendly. Sartre uses the same word, *trop*, that we saw him using in *Nausea* to express this human superfluity.

The customers in the café tend to reduce the waiter to his occupation, whereas the waiter necessarily transcends this attempt to limit his possibilities by virtue of the structure of consciousness. Sartre sets out this structure when he supplies what amounts to a new account of consciousness that is significantly different from that we found in 'Intentionality', where consciousness was described as a bursting out. In *Being and Nothingness* it comes to be understood as a nothingness. This arises from Sartre's revised understanding of intentionality in a more Heideggerian vein: the directedness of consciousness towards objects is made possible by consciousness's transcendence, its power to see objects in the light of its own possibilities that it projects into the future. In other words, consciousness sees things in a particular light because of its project which surpasses current reality and, in so doing, approaches it through a kind of negation. I see the world in terms of what it could be because I see it not in terms of what I am but in terms of what I could be.

Nevertheless, one needs to be absolutely clear that Sartre is not denying that the person who brings me my drink is a waiter. My Manhattan is not served to me by someone who is masquerading as a waiter. The waiter plays at being a waiter, as opposed to imitating waiters for amusement, because he or she is a waiter. The key term in Sartre's description of the waiter is the word 'realize'. The waiter plays at being a waiter in order to 'realize' this condition. The term is used in a technical sense. A good guide to how Sartre is using the term is found in the conclusion of *The Imaginary*, a text that he cites in the above extract. Sartre there argued that a painter does not first have a mental image which he or she then realizes on the canvas: the materials that the painter uses are real, but, by contrast, the work of art itself is an irreal object. Or, to use a more illuminating example, the actor who plays Hamlet uses his feelings as analogues of the feelings of Hamlet, but however much the actor is gripped by the part, Hamlet is not being realized by the actor. It is still an actor on the stage, not Hamlet. That is why, instead of saying that Hamlet is realized, Sartre says that the actor is being irrealized in the character in the sense of being brought to live in an entirely irreal or make-believe world. Things are different with this man who plays at being a waiter because, as Sartre says, we are dealing with real existences. Nevertheless, for himself, the waiter can never be reduced to being a waiter. Sartre calls this 'an irrealizable', by which he means that however much I am for my customers a waiter, for myself I am not one, not least because I can always quit tomorrow and because I do this job only to meet my other needs.

Sartre believes that what he has shown with respect to the waiter is true not only for all occupations, but also for one's rationality, one's appearance, one's class, one's race and characteristics – like being vulgar – or states of consciousness, like being sad. We can strive to be these things only because we are for ourselves none of these things simply and without remainder. Soon after he gives the example of the waiter, Sartre offers the example of being sad. He describes the look and the way of carrying oneself that goes with being sad, but comments that in the very moment of adopting this way of being we know that we will be unable to stay sad indefinitely. As soon as someone comes to see us, then, as likely as not, we will adopt a cheerful attitude, all the while making an appointment with ourselves to resume our sadness the moment our visitor leaves. In other words, ultimately we make ourselves sad, and we continue to do so as long as the mood lasts. And if we must make ourselves sad, that means we are not sad in the way that this chair is a chair.

Sartre argues that if every human being was simply identical with itself – if it was itself and nothing but itself – then bad faith would be impossible. That means that the condition of possibility of bad faith is that I am not what I am. Or, in a famous formulation: 'Consciousness is what it is not and is not what it is.' Sartre's theory of consciousness accounts for bad faith, but it turns sincerity into a problem. For sincerity to be possible, a human being would have to be identical to him- or herself, or, in Sartre's terms, it would have to be a thing. The upshot of Sartre's account is that sincerity, at least as ordinarily conceived, is an inappropriate demand because it ignores the very character of human existence. It seems that Sartre, by explaining the possibility of bad faith, rules out sincerity unless he can show the possibility of some kind of self-recovery.

In a footnote at the end of the chapter, Sartre calls this self-recovery 'authenticity', but he postpones discussion of it, never to return to it in his published writings except for a few passing references, such as those we find in *Anti-Semite and Jew*. The unpublished *Notebooks for an Ethics* offer the most extended discussion, but it is still hard not to reach the conclusion that bad faith has been rendered possible only by sacrificing – or at very least postponing to a world in which human relations are very different – the possibility of sincerity. In so far as authenticity seems to await a change in society, then what might initially look like an ethical condition – the obligation to be what we are – necessarily awaits a political transformation. Sartre's subsequent turn to politics is therefore entirely in keeping with his philosophical discovery of bad faith in *Being and Nothingness*.

I have said that Sartre highlights the excessive character of the waiter's behaviour in an attempt to show how the waiter, even as he is reduced to being a waiter and nothing more by the customers of the café who are oblivious to him, nevertheless escapes this imposition. To explicate this process more precisely Sartre employs the terms 'transcendence' and 'facticity' that he borrows from Heidegger but employs in his own distinctive sense. By 'facticity' Heidegger means the 'that it is' of human existence. Sartre uses the same term to describe the facts about me that limit me: my history, my gender, race, nationality, class, appearance, and so on. Transcendence, my self-surpassing, is inseparable from facticity; it supplies facticity with meaning in such a way that one cannot tell where transcendence and facticity each begin and end: this is the central ambiguity at the heart of Sartre's account of human existence. It enables him to insist that one can never grasp facticity in its brute existence, its basic nudity. This will prove important when we turn to the task of understanding Sartre's account of freedom in the next chapter.

5

'IN WAR THERE ARE NO INNOCENT VICTIMS'

Sartre was not the kind of philosopher who formulated balanced or even anodyne truth-claims that were appropriately qualified to command universal assent. He spoke the language of overstatement, and even when he corrected one overstatement it was usually by saying something equally extravagant in the other direction. His aim was to provoke thought, and he was never more provocative than in the extract below where, beginning from his insistence that we are all totally free, he drew the conclusion that there are no innocent victims of war.

The essential consequence of our earlier remarks is that man being condemned to be free carries the weight of the whole world on his shoulders; he is responsible for the world and for himself as a way of being. We are taking the word 'responsibility' in its ordinary sense as 'consciousness (of) being the incontestable author of an event or of an object.' In this sense the responsibility of the for-itself is overwhelming since he is the one by whom it happens that *there is* a world; since he is also the one who makes himself be, then whatever may be the situation in which he finds himself, the for-itself must wholly assume this situation with its peculiar coefficient of adversity, even though it be insupportable. Is it not I who decides the coefficient of adversity in things and even their unpre- dictability by deciding myself?

Thus there are no *accidents* in a life; a community event which suddenly bursts forth and involves me in it does not come from the outside. If I am mobilized in a war, this war is *my* war; it is in my image and I deserve it. I deserve it first because I could always get out of it by suicide or by desertion; these ultimate possibles are those which must always be pres- ent for us when there is a question of envisaging a situation. For lack of getting out of it, I have *chosen* it. This can be due to inertia, to cowardice in the face of public opinion, or because I prefer certain other values to the value of the refusal to join in the war (the good opinion of my relatives, the honour of my family, etc.). Anyway you look at it, it is a matter of choice. This choice will be repeated later on again and again without a break until the end of the war. Therefore we must agree with the statement by J. Romains, 'In war there are no innocent victims.' If therefore I have preferred war to death or to dishonour, everything takes place as if I bore the entire responsibility for this war. [. . .]

But in addition the war is *mine* because by the sole fact that it arises in a situation which I cause to be and that I can discover it there only by engaging myself for or against it, I can no longer distinguish at present the choice which I make of myself from the choice which I make of the war. To live this war is to choose myself through it and to choose it through my choice of myself. [. . .]

Finally, [. . .] I have chosen myself as one of the possible meanings of the epoch which imperceptibly led to war. I am not distinct from this same epoch; I could not be transported to another epoch without contradiction. Thus I *am* this war which restricts and limits and makes comprehensible the period which preceded it. In this sense we may define more precisely the responsibility of the for-itself if to the earlier quoted statement, 'There are no innocent victims,' we add the words, 'We have the war we deserve.' Thus, totally free, undistinguishable from the period for which I have chosen to be the meaning, as profoundly responsible for the war as if I had myself declared it, unable to live without integrating it in *my* situation, engaging myself in it wholly and stamping it with my seal, I must be without remorse or regrets as I am without excuse; for from the instant of my upsurge into being, I carry the weight of the world by myself alone without anything or any person being able to lighten it.

Being and Nothingness

The above may sound almost as bad as Hegel's account of history as a court of judgement: 'No people ever suffered wrong; what it suffered, it had merited.'[1] The fact that when, in 1943, Sartre wrote the above he was not fully aware of the true horrors going on around him cannot be an excuse. I cannot justify his refusal to acknowledge the existence of innocent victims at this time, but it is at least possible to give some indication of how he came to write it. I shall begin by showing that he cannot hide behind his attribution of it to Jules Romains, as he attempts to do.

In late November 1939, Sartre, who had been called up to the army as a member of the Meteorological Corps, was reading Jules Romains' novels *Verdun. The Prelude* and *Verdun. The Battle*. Romains was regarded as one of the great literary figures of France at that time and his two books on Verdun, which were part of the novel series *Men of Good Will* that eventually ran to twenty-seven volumes, had just been published in the previous year. They provide a vivid portrait of one of the bloodiest battles of the First World War, told both on the grand scale and at the level of the individual. The central character, Jean Jerphanion, is a lieutenant in the infantry and during a brief period of leave in Paris he discusses with his close friend, Pierre Jallez, both the battle and the contempt that soldiers at the front feel for civilians and soldiers with soft jobs. Jallez observes that the soldiers were not simply pitiable victims of someone else's folly: they had once been civilians and had played their part in the stupidity that led to war. By way of agreement Jerphanion utters the sentence that Sartre subsequently misquotes: 'War claims many victims, but very few of them are innocent.'[2] Already when Sartre cites this sentence in his *War Diaries* he misquotes in a way that modifies it considerably: he generalizes so that he has Romains say that in war there are *no* innocent victims.[3] He misquotes it in *Being and Nothingness* in the same form (and wrongly attributes it there to *Verdun: The Prelude* instead of *Verdun: The Battle*). Furthermore, he ignores the context of the sentence, obscuring the fact that in the novel Jerphanion expresses his loathing for his fellow-men and the further observation that those who are most to blame usually do not suffer the worst punishment. In this way Sartre takes what is intended as an expression of political outrage and disgust and turns it into a philosophical thesis. The way in which he misquotes this short phrase takes us to the heart of what appears to be a central ambiguity of his philosophy of freedom: the passage between his ontological idea of freedom and his political theory of freedom. This passage between them will be the focus of the next two chapters. It would occupy Sartre for the remainder of his life.

The definitive formulation of Sartre's ontological position

on freedom as it is presented in *Being and Nothingness* is that 'I am condemned to be free'. When Sartre introduced this formula he explained that it meant that freedom is without limits except for the fact that we are not free to cease being free. However, he subsequently added that the sentence could be paraphrased in Heidegger's language by the formula 'we are thrown into freedom', or 'we are abandoned to freedom'. In other words, Sartre was not within this formula highlighting freedom at the expense of facticity, which is how it has sometimes been taken. He was rather highlighting the facticity at the heart of freedom, recalling that to be free does not mean to get what one wants but simply that one is responsible for what one wants. Freedom for Sartre does not mean success in one's projects, but only that one gets to choose one's projects.

This is highlighted by the passing reference to 'the coefficient of adversity' in the above extract. The phrase 'coefficient of adversity' has its source in Gaston Bachelard's (1884–1962) *Waters and Dreams*, an essay first published in 1942, the year before *Being and Nothingness*. Bachelard argued that the philosopher places reality on a firm foundation only when he or she approaches matter of whatever kind in terms of the human labour that it calls for. Bachelard complained that on these terms the phenomenological doctrine of intentionality was too formal or intellectual to accord to objects in the world 'their true coefficient of adversity'. In *Being and Nothingness*, Sartre explicitly sought to develop a phenomenology that could withstand this criticism, while conceding that it justly characterized his phenomenological predecessors. It is important to understand the way he did so.

Sartre took up Bachelard's suggestion that the philosopher should focus on instrumentality. Sartre located instrumentality primarily in the body in all its facticity. His point, which he applied to all aspects of facticity, including race, class and nationality (we might wonder why he so rarely includes sex), is that one's facticity is not perceived directly but is discovered in the world as one negotiates the obstacles to one's projects. For example, I discover my ugliness by the unwelcome reaction it provokes rather than by looking in the mirror. To be sure, the fact that Sartre frequently suggests, as he does in the above extract, that I am the one who decides the coefficient of adversity of things lends support to those who would argue that Sartre still did not give sufficient weight to the obstacles to freedom. It is a point that Sartre himself readily conceded many years later in interviews, albeit in that somewhat exaggerated way that I mentioned earlier. It is important to look beyond such rhetorical flourishes to find the philosophical basis for the position outlined in *Being and Nothingness*.

At its simplest, Sartre is saying that my freedom to choose my goals or projects entails that I have also chosen the obstacles I encounter along the way. It is by deciding to climb this mountain that I have turned the weakness of my body and the steepness of the cliffs into obstacles, which they were not so long as I was content simply to gaze at the mountain from the comfort of my chair. Of course, if this is what Sartre is saying, then he would seem to be only one step away from advocating a vulgar form of Stoicism, whereby one restricts one's desires so as not to be disappointed. However, Sartre's philosophy of commitment in fact sends him in a completely different direction.

This takes place through Sartre's somewhat idiosyncratic understanding of Heidegger's account of the thrown project. At this time Sartre highlights one-sidedly the contribution of projection of possibilities to the neglect of an equal appreciation of thrownness or facticity. Because my projection of my possibilities of existence determines my situation and the way things appear, then, in so far as I decide or determine my project, it would seem to follow that there is a sense in which I not only choose my projects but in the process choose my world. We saw this with the example of the mountain, which could be either an obstacle or an object of my aesthetic pleasure depending on my project. It is by extending the argument to cover the world and not just those specific things that have been turned into obstacles or advantages as a result of my choice of a project that Sartre gives the argument the political twist that emerges in the above extract. It is in so far as I choose my world that it becomes possible for Sartre to say that each of us is responsible for whatever takes place there, even a war. Indeed, we read above Sartre saying that I am responsible for the war as if I had declared the war myself.

Sartre's argument for this in the passage cited above proceeds by stages. At first the claim seems to be simply that if I go to war and do not become a deserter or a pacifist, then I have accepted it. To that extent I am faced with a choice. It may well be that the fact that there is this war was not up to me, but denying that there is one will not bring about peace. What is up to me is the attitude that I take towards the war and this is what determines my war and the way it impacts upon me. It is here that Sartre comes closest to what might ordinarily be meant by saying that there are no innocent victims. In the final analysis there is always suicide. Suicide does not make me any more or less superfluous, as Sartre explained in *Nausea*, but the possibility of suicide means that by choosing to stay alive I have chosen this world, at least in so far as I could have refused to live in it.

However, in a second stage of the argument Sartre applies the lessons he has learned from Heidegger. Because I have no access to things in the world independent of my relation to them, at a fundamental level I will never be able to say definitively what I bring to them and what they provide. That is to say, because there is no clear dividing line between transcendence and facticity, as we already saw in the previous chapter, then I cannot clearly separate what my project contributes to the way I see the situation from what belongs to the facticity of the situation. This means, in a further step in the argument, that my choice of myself and my choice of the war are one and the same choice. Ultimately I am this situation in which I find myself, and in choosing myself I have chosen it.

This argument is accompanied by a corresponding transformation in the notion of responsibility. Sartre initially tells the reader that he is employing the word 'responsibility' in the sense that one is responsible for something only if one is its 'incontestable author'. However, within two pages he has drawn an extraordinary conclusion: 'I am responsible for everything, in fact, except my very responsibility.' Sartre was even more forthright in an unpublished manuscript from 1948 where he wrote that it belongs to the nature of freedom that it assumes responsibility afterwards, even for what one neither created nor wanted.[4] However, responsibility is not primarily backward looking. I take responsibility for the past only by choosing a future. That is why responsibility does not mean accountability. Nor does it imply culpability. It is through this hyperbolic sense of responsibility that Sartre will later tie his ontological conception of freedom, according to which I am free by nature, to his political conception of freedom as something that needs to be brought about. It is thus through reference to responsibility that Sartre combats the possibility of his philosophy of freedom lapsing into a kind of Stoic indifferentism in which I adapt to the hand

I have been dealt rather than trying to make something of it.

This aspect of Sartre's philosophy should always be understood as part of his response to the German occupation of Paris. The following year, soon after the liberation in 1944, Sartre declared in a radio address on the BBC: 'We were never more free than during the German Occupation.'[5] Nothing better indicates the complex interplay between ontological and political freedom in Sartre than this sentence. Ontologically there are no degrees of freedom: we are all totally free all of the time. Politically there are degrees of freedom, but instead of measuring these in terms of one's rights, for example to free speech or to free movement, Sartre looked to the extent to which the question of freedom is posed. Under the Nazi occupation the French found the conventional freedoms that they had taken for granted curtailed. Nevertheless, these same circumstances led every French person to think about resistance and about how they might respond under torture, and this made freedom real. The occupation posed the question of freedom not as an issue of the simple possibility of choosing one thing over another, but as an issue of social responsibility to be expressed in actions undertaken in the face of death. The political circumstances that might lead us to retreat into a kind of inner freedom can also provoke us to action.

Why then did Sartre insist so strenuously on an ontological account according to which to exist is to be totally free, if what he really was aiming for was for us to take responsibility for our lack of freedom and thereby oblige us to fight for it? A full answer to this question will have to await subsequent chapters, but a provisional answer can be given here. Sartre deduces his politics of freedom from metaphysical freedom, the claim that 'I am totally free.' Or, more simply expressed, it is because freedom belongs to me by virtue of my existence that my lack of freedom in the world is a scandal that I must try to correct. Sartre's focus on ontology in *Being and Nothingness* is therefore not a distraction from the scandal of oppressive material conditions but the basis on which he would address them. To be sure, the aim of Sartre's philosophy was, as he had already indicated in the essay on intentionality, to arrive at the concrete. He believed that to do so one must begin from the abstract and employ description. Thus his starting point, as we have seen, was the abstract dualism between consciousness as being-for-itself and being-in-itself. However, while he looked to his descriptions not so much to support this division as to correct or overcome it, at the same time he looked to the ontology to offer a guide as to how to conceive our priorities. To that extent he was fully justified to close *Being and Nothingness* with a discussion of the ethical implications of the book. Nevertheless, even though he makes clear that he will address the ethical issues in terms of responsibility, he did not yet have a clear awareness of the following question, let alone an answer: 'Before whom am I responsible?' However, as we shall see later, by the mid-1950s, when he introduces the idea of the gaze of the least favoured, he will have, and the ethics of responsibility will become a politics against oppression.

6

'I AM OBLIGED TO WANT OTHERS TO HAVE FREEDOM'

When Sartre delivered the lecture 'Existentialism Is a Humanism' in Paris on 28 October 1945, so many people gathered to hear it that chairs were broken, people fainted and Sartre could scarcely be heard. At that time existentialism was not yet well understood, but interest in it was overwhelming. And yet only two months earlier Sartre had refused to adopt the label 'existentialism' when Gabriel Marcel had applied it to his writings, preferring Heidegger's phrase 'philosophy of existence'. However, he was too good a self-publicist to continue with this stance once interest in existentialism gathered momentum. 'Existentialism is a Humanism' was therefore Sartre's first major attempt to clarify what he himself meant by the term 'existentialism.'

> Atheistic existentialism, which I represent, [. . .] states that if God does not exist, there is at least one being in whom existence precedes essence, a being who exists before he can be defined by any concept, and that this being is man, or, as Heidegger says, human reality. What is meant here by saying that existence precedes essence? It means that, first of all,

man exists, turns up, appears on the scene, and, only afterwards, defines himself. If man, as the existentialist conceives him, is indefinable, it is because at first he is nothing. Only afterward will he be something, and he himself will have made what he will be. [. . .]

Existentialism's first move is to make every man aware of what he is and to make the full responsibility of his existence rest on him. And when we say that a man is responsible for himself, we do not only mean that he is responsible for his own individuality, but that he is responsible for all men. [. . .]

When we say that man chooses his own self, we mean that every one of us does likewise; but we also mean by that that in making this choice he also chooses all men. In fact, in creating the man that we want to be, there is not a single one of our acts which does not at the same time create an image of man as we think he ought to be. To choose to be this or that is to affirm at the same time the value of what we choose, because we can never choose evil. We always choose the good, and nothing can be good for us without being good for all. [. . .]

When I declare that freedom in every concrete circumstance can have no other aim than to want itself, if man has once become aware that in his forlornness he imposes values, he can no longer want but one thing, and that is freedom, as the basis of all values. [. . .] [T]his freedom is wanted in something concrete. We want freedom for freedom's sake and in every particular circumstance. And in wanting freedom we discover that it depends entirely on the freedom of others, and that the freedom of others depends on ours. Of course, freedom as the definition of man does not depend on others, but as soon as there is involvement, I am obliged to want others to have freedom at the same time that I want my own freedom.

I can take freedom as my goal only if I take that of others as a goal as well.

'Existentialism is a Humanism'

It has been widely reported that Sartre renounced this work, but it seems that the only direct evidence for this claim is François Jeanson's assertion in *Sartre and the Problem of Morality* that Sartre regarded the lecture as an 'error', in so far as readers relying on it exclusively would have a basis for complaining that he had advocated 'a quite empty pseudo-morality'.[1] However, Sartre deeply regretted that it was this lecture, of all his theoretical works, that was the one that had the broadest circulation.[2] He believed that, read in isolation, it gave a misleading idea of existentialism. It was never intended as a manifesto, but merely as an opportunity to try out some ideas about the moral dimension of existentialism. Perhaps more significant is the fact that Sartre used the opportunity of the lecture to answer his critics, especially those who were suspicious that his philosophy lacked an ethical import.

Sartre's problem was that his ideas on ethics were still only in their infancy. He had introduced the section 'Freedom and Responsibility' in *Being and Nothingness* by saying that it would interest the moralists, and he concluded the book with two pages of 'ethical implications', but the ethical and political ramifications of the book remained undeveloped. 'Existentialism is a Humanism' changed that. The lecture does not serve as a manifesto for existentialism, which is unfortunately how it is usually treated. It *does* show Sartre highlighting ethics. He employs the argument from *Being and Nothingness* that to be condemned to freedom is to be responsible for the world and he extends it into an argument for the somewhat vague, but nevertheless stunning, claim that nobody is free unless all are free. This does not give us much ethical guidance. Indeed, by suggesting, as he does, that there is no place for guidance or prescriptions, because one simply chooses as an adviser someone who will say what one wants to hear, he gives his readers the impression that existentialist morality is empty. However, there was nothing empty about Sartre's political commitment to freedom for all. For this reason the lecture is an excellent introduction to Sartre's politics in so far as it establishes the basis of that politics.

The full text of the lecture makes it clear that, as in *Being and Nothingness*, Sartre's argument operates in terms of the notion of Heidegger's project. However, he also constantly reiterates in the lecture the significance of Heidegger's notion of 'abandonment' (*Überlassenheit*), a word which appears in the above extract translated as 'forlornness' and which highlights the sense in which the human being exists only in having chosen to make a choice. Nevertheless, although this makes Sartre's philosophy seem to have moved closer to Heidegger's philosophy in *Being and Time*, there is still a gulf separating them.

This was reflected in Heidegger's 'Letter on Humanism', where he responds to Sartre's claim that existence precedes essence. Heidegger's criticism that Sartre had merely reversed the Western metaphysical tradition – which since Plato had privileged essence – was based on the assumption that Sartre was using the terms 'existence' and 'essence' in their traditional sense. However, it seems clear that Sartre was using the terms differently. When he says 'man exists', he explains that he means by it that human beings propel themselves towards a future and are conscious of doing so. When Sartre says that 'existence precedes essence' he means that human beings are primarily futural and not to be defined by what they have been or done, as Hegel (1770–1831) had done when he wrote that 'essence is what has been'. In saying that 'existence precedes essence' Sartre rewrites Heidegger's claim that 'the essence of *Dasein* is existence' so that it means that the essence of human reality is freedom, and, most importantly, in a sense of the term 'freedom' that is directed ultimately toward political freedom.

When, towards the end of the extract, Sartre describes freedom as the definition of man, it may seem that the very idea of a definition of man runs counter to the claim that existence precedes essence: is not to define the human being to revert to traditional ideas of 'the essence of man'? Sartre's argument would be that it belongs to the nature of freedom alone that it avoids this problem because it describes a fundamental openness that is limited only by the impossibility of choosing not to be free. Furthermore, he employs his definition of man to secure the passage from what I earlier called ontological freedom to political or concrete freedom: although freedom as the definition of man does not depend on ethics, as soon as there is involvement or, more precisely, commitment, my pursuit of my own freedom obliges me to work for the freedom of all.

One part of Sartre's argument in the above extract is that by our actions we not only seek to realize ourselves but also create an image of what humanity ought to be. Our choice of ourselves through a choice of a project is a choice of a 'type of humanity', as he says later in the lecture. This image or type functions like Aristotle's *phronimos*, the person who exhibits practical reasoning by doing the right thing at the right time and thereby exemplifying human virtue in the sense of human excellence. Sartre is not saying that we should as a matter of ethics act as if others were to imitate our actions; he is simply recognizing that to act is necessarily to create an image for humanity to follow. For example, to choose to get married is not to say everyone should be married, but it is to support the institution of marriage. Every agent by their actions promotes a type of existence.

Sartre's point is so deceptively simple that most commentators appear to have missed it. We always choose; even not choosing is still a choice. Furthermore, we always choose what we consider the best option under the circumstances. We may choose the lesser of two evils, we may not be comfortable with the choice we are faced with, but it is still chosen by us as the best in the circumstance. Philosophers are more familiar with Immanuel Kant's (1724–1804) argument that we *should* choose only what we can will to be a universal law. For example, the Kantian argues that we should not steal because we would not want to live in a world in which someone is liable to steal from us what we have just taken from another. Sartre's argument is somewhat different: he is saying that by choosing to steal I have chosen a world in which property is not secure.

However, the important point to recognize is that Sartre does not stop there. He introduces this argument only as a prelude to asking what it is we all choose, and his predictable answer is freedom. Whenever we choose, we inevitably choose freedom, in so far as any choice is an expression of freedom and even not choosing is a choice. For Sartre, it is only from the ontological claim that the human being *is* a freedom that one can proceed to a discussion of whether or not someone is concretely free. It is, as he says in the *Notebooks for an Ethics*, because man is free that oppression has a meaning.[3] This is why Sartre's ontology of freedom is not a luxury that can be sacrificed for a more streamlined political philosophy that omits the abstract ontology and starts immediately with concrete description, as Merleau-Ponty sought to do in his *Phenomenology of Perception*. It is only because humans have this ontological characteristic that the question of bringing one's concrete existence into line with it by becoming concretely free arises as an obligation.

The relation between the ontological claim that I am condemned to be free by virtue of my very existence and the argument that 'nobody is free unless all are free' seems to cause a great deal of confusion even among some of Sartre's best commentators. The ontological claim does not exclude but motivates concern about the freedom of others, or even my own freedom. It is because I am free by virtue of being human that my factual lack of freedom and that of all others is a scandal.

Freedom is the value we invariably exemplify and, in so far as in choosing for oneself one chooses for all, by pursuing freedom we are fashioning an image of ourselves that promotes freedom for all. In this way, 'Existentialism is a Humanism' gives rise to a politics of freedom where freedom is not to be realized for only half of mankind while they enslave the other half, but where freedom is for all. That is why one must beware of taking Sartre's claim here that our being free depends on the freedom of others as a practical argument. As such, it would seem at most to establish the freedom of some, but not the freedom of all. With the phrase 'freedom as the definition of man' he is referring to what I have been calling ontological freedom. It is concrete freedom that needs others to be free.

Sartre believes that we are in bad faith if we do not seek freedom for all, because it amounts to deceiving ourselves about the nature of freedom. In other words, oppression is based on a fundamental error. That is why Sartre's philosophy emerges as entirely alien to the ideology of the oppressing class and at the same time highly plausible to the oppressed. Indeed, this has been the history of its reception, which has been most pronounced in the Third World.

To put it another way, one cannot in Sartre's view be authentic on one's own for the simple reason that one is fundamentally always in relation to others. In this way, the cult of individual authenticity that is often associated with existentialism, not to mention the other problems of trying to give an account of authenticity in the context of a framework that accommodates bad faith, as mentioned in an earlier chapter, is dismissed at a stroke. Because freedom is the meaning of what it is to be human, to recognize other human beings in their humanity is to recognize them in, and so promote, their freedom. From the moment that Sartre elucidates the structures of bad faith, not just in terms of the relation one has with oneself, but the relation one has with others, his philosophy has set out a path that can only complete itself by arguing for changing society. And yet even in 'Existentialism is a Humanism' this argument is not formulated explicitly, but is only hinted at in the form of the statement declaring 'I can want only the freedom of others.' It first becomes explicit in *Anti-Semite and Jew*.

7

'THE AUTHENTIC JEW MAKES HIMSELF A JEW'

[The Jew's] life is nothing but a long flight from others and from himself. He has been alienated even from his own body; his emotional life has been cut in two; he has been reduced to pursuing the impossible dream of universal brotherhood in a world that rejects him.

Whose is the fault? It is our eyes that reflect to him the unacceptable image that he wishes to dissimulate. It is our words and our gestures – *all* our words and *all* our gestures – our anti-Semitism, but equally our condescending liberalism – that have poisoned him. It is we who constrain him to choose to be a Jew whether through flight from himself or through self-assertion; it is we who force him into the dilemma of Jewish authenticity or inauthenticity. [. . .] In this situation there is not one of us who is not totally guilty and even criminal; the Jewish blood that the Nazis shed falls on all our heads.

The fact remains, you may answer, that the Jew is free: he can choose to be authentic. That is true, but we must understand first of all that *that does not concern us*. The prisoner is always free to try to run away, if it is clearly understood that he risks death in crawling under the barbed wire. Is his jailer any less guilty on that account? [. . .]

The inauthentic Jew flees Jewish reality, and the anti-Semite makes him a Jew in spite of himself; but the authentic Jew *makes himself a Jew*, in the face of all and against all. He accepts all, even martyrdom, and the anti-Semite, deprived of his weapons, must be content to yelp at the Jew as he goes by, and can no longer touch him.

Thus the choice of authenticity appears to be a *moral* decision, bringing certainty to the Jew on the ethical level but in no way serving as a solution on the social or political level: the situation of the Jew is such that everything he does turns against him.

Anti-Semite and Jew

Sartre wrote *Anti-Semite and Jew* in 1944, before the end of the war. The following year he published its first part, a portrait of the anti-Semite, but he withheld most of the text on the advice of some Jewish friends. Because the first part was well received, Sartre relented and published the whole text in 1946. Initially it too found an enthusiastic audience. In particular, it was welcomed by Jews who were struck by the fact that, in the aftermath of the Holocaust, the existence of French anti-Semitism was being over-looked in an attempt to maintain the pretence of French unity. However, Sartre might subsequently have wished he had kept the second part to himself. As he himself conceded many years later, after the criticisms grew, he knew next to nothing about Jewish history at this time, and his ignorance led him to make some outrageous claims. In particular, he suggested the Jewish community was not a concrete historical community, but only an abstract one, and that, as a consequence of the diaspora, it did not have a historic past.

Sartre's ignorance of Jewish history when he wrote the book has been justly criticized. As a result of this failing, his account of the Jew is deeply flawed, but one should not overlook the fact that that was not Sartre's primary focus. It is no accident that this criticism was first widely voiced in the United States of America, where the English-language title given to Sartre's book may have led readers to expect a portrait of the Jew as a counterbalance to the portrait of the anti-Semite. But that was never Sartre's intention. To be sure, the title *Anti-Semite and Jew* must have been chosen by the English-language publishers because of embarrassment at the French title, a literal translation of which would be *Reflections on the Jewish Question*. This phrase is clearly a provocation because of the long history of its use in anti-Semitic literature. Sartre used the title as a basis for his insistence that the so-called Jewish problem was actually what one might call a 'Gentile problem', just as the so-called black problem in the United States was in fact, as Richard Wright had told Sartre, a white problem. However, there are deeper problems with the text that go beyond Sartre's ignorance of Jewish history or the difficulty of finding an appropriate title. It was presumptuous of Sartre to describe the alternatives facing Jews in France at that time. However, he wanted to show that they had no good options, not in order to criticize them or to dismiss their choices, but primarily to provide a backdrop to his conclusion that a radical change in the situation offered the only way of addressing the problems created by anti-Semitism. Certainly he should have had more to say about Jews in a book about anti-Semitism. Given his lack of knowledge, we can perhaps be glad that he did not. However, he should be judged on the basis of what he was attempting to do, as well as condemned for his lamentable and surprising ignorance.

It must be said that Sartre's portrait of the anti-Semite was equally unencumbered, so far as one can see, by anything that remotely resembles historical research. However, the fact that his portrait of the anti-Semite is as thoroughly penetrating and devastating as his portrait of the Jew is flat and abstract, means that the former has not been exposed to as much critical attention as the latter. Sartre's idea that anti-Semitism is a prejudice that arises from mediocrity is hardly new, but his conviction that one cannot be an anti-Semite alone, that one embraces anti-Semitism to be a member of a community of the mediocre, has genuine merit. Sartre develops this idea further in later works in the context of his analysis of the racist basis of colonialism, as I will document later. Sartre refuses to see anti-Semitism as caused by external factors. It is a passion and an all-encompassing choice of both oneself and the world. In other words, anti-Semitism is not a contingent feature about someone. That means that one cannot reasonably conduct a thought experiment in which one uses analysis to subtract that anti-Semitism from one's image of that person so that one could then go on to say that one admires that person apart from his or her anti-Semitism. Anti-Semitism embraces the whole personality of the anti-Semite. This shows just how far Sartre is from thinking through this topic analytically. Sartre goes so far as to deny the anti-Semite the right to express his or her views. Although he does not spell out the argument, it would seem that his claim is, following 'Existentialism is a Humanism', that this freedom of the anti-Semite is a false freedom because it does not strive for the freedom of all.

But there is a further, even more telling, example of this

when it comes to Sartre's critique of the Enlightenment conviction that the best resource with which to fight anti-Semitism is a belief in the universality of 'man'. Sartre had initially taken the Enlightenment position as his own. He presented it in an interview he gave in 1939 on anti-Semitism, but his interviewer, who was a Jew, objected that he did not want to be respected as a man, but as a Jew. In *Anti-Semite and Jew* Sartre presented the Enlightenment position on 'man' as a flawed result of analytical thinking. Sartre's answer to that position is the same as that of Joseph de Maistre (1753–1821). De Maistre proclaimed that 'there is no such thing as *man* in the world. I have seen Frenchmen, Italians, Russians, etc.; thanks to Montesquieu, I even know that *one can be Persian*. But as for *man*, I declare that I have never in my life met him; if he exists, he is unknown to me.'[1] The 'friend of the Jew' who defends the Jew as 'a man' sacrifices the Jew's Jewishness and thus seems, like the anti-Semite, to want the Jew as Jew to disappear. This is why Sartre in the first paragraph of the extract describes the dilemma of the Jew as one of being caught between 'the impossible dream' of universal brotherhood and a world that rejects Jews.

It is entirely typical of Sartre that he does not use this diagnosis of the anti-Semite to distance himself from it so as to establish his good conscience. Instead, he acknowledges his own complicity – 'our anti-Semitism' – in the dilemma that faces Jews as they try to negotiate a world that sets out to persecute them. We see here the impact of Sartre's account of responsibility introduced in *Being and Nothingness*. It is our responsibility and our failure to act that makes anti-Semites of us all.

This helps to explain the most famous claim to emerge from *Anti-Semite and Jew*: 'the anti-Semite makes the Jew'. Sartre employs this phrase to summarize a series of claims, some of which have more merit than others. One of the ways in which the anti-Semite makes the Jew is through the gaze that reduces the Jew to an object. Jews, like other persecuted people, can under certain circumstances come to see themselves through the eyes of others. This is the basis for the phenomenon sometimes describes as 'self-hatred'. By contrast, other Jews try to deprive anti-Semitism of its weapons by making themselves Jews. These are the Jews Sartre called 'authentic'. Sartre often had recourse to the term 'authenticity' that he inherited from Heidegger, but it was a constant source of problems for him. Up until this point in his career he had had very little to say in print about the nature of authenticity. The few remarks he did make in *Anti-Semite and Jew* do not seem to have done much to help. He explains that to be authentic one must be conscious of the situation one finds oneself in and assume the responsibilities it involves. However, he acknowledges that even though the authentic Jew and the inauthentic Jew relate differently to the situation in which all Jews find themselves, this difference does not resolve the problem. The situation itself is, as he puts it, a false one. However, this does not mean that Sartre is reserving authenticity for non-Jews. There are, on his account, at least as many obstacles in the way of a Christian seeking authenticity.

Sartre also insists that if the Jew did not exist, the anti-Semite would invent him. This claim invites us to look at the anti-Semite rather than the Jew for an explanation of anti-Semitism as a phenomenon, and it also points in the direction of a link between anti-Semitism, racism and perhaps also other forms of hatred. Sartre suggested that in the absence of Jews, the anti-Semite would target another group. Furthermore, it is a merit of the claim that if there were no Jews the anti-

Semite would be compelled to invent them that it acknowledges the existence of Jews independently of anti-Semites.
However, some of Sartre's readers attribute to him an extreme
and perhaps ultimately incoherent form of social construc-
tionism according to which there would be no Jews if the
anti-Semite had not invented them. Sartre's philosophy was an
inspiration to the social constructionists, who believe that
much that had been believed to be natural, such as race, was
in fact a product of society. However, Sartre himself makes a
different point: he believes that we are fundamentally unable
to determine what is given by nature and what is added to it
by society.

In the above extract, drawn from the third of the book's
four sections, Sartre returns to the portrait of the anti-Semite
with which his essay had begun, but there is now a decisive
difference in his approach. Instead of isolating the anti-Semite
as a being apart, different from the rest of us, as he does at the
beginning of the book, Sartre now argues that the ordinary
French person is also implicated in this same anti-Semitism. In
Black Skin, White Masks Frantz Fanon (1925–61) quotes
extensively from the same pages from which this extract is
drawn, calling them the finest pages he had ever read: 'the
finest, because the problems discussed in them grips us in our
guts'.[2] Fanon uses Sartre's analysis of anti-Semitism as a basis
for his own account of anti-black racism, just as he allows his
discussion of the options facing blacks to be partially moulded
by Sartre's discussion of the authentic and the inauthentic
Jew. Fanon is ultimately highly critical of Sartre's account in
'Black Orpheus' that envisages a time when blacks will be
called upon to renounce their racial identity as a preparation
for a classless society. Nevertheless, because Fanon's response
to Sartre's vision of a race-free future is couched not as an out-

right rejection, but with the words 'I needed not to know', there is still a certain ambiguity about Fanon's own position.

Sartre indicates that it is only in a classless society that anti-Semitism might disappear altogether and that only then would assimilation become a genuine possibility. Exactly what assimilation amounts to here is not altogether clear. If it means that the Jew is asked to renounce his or her Jewishness, in the same way that Sartre asks blacks to renounce their negritude as a prelude to a classless society, in 'Black Orpheus', then it would mean that Sartre's proposal does not allow for the preservation of Jewish identity. That conforms to what one might expect, if the anti-Semite indeed makes the Jew. However, Sartre is not insensitive in the final section of *Anti-Semite and Jew* to the fact that French Jews want to integrate themselves into France as *Jews*. Ultimately, there is a fair degree of ambiguity surrounding Sartre's relation to the future of Jewish identity, as there is with Fanon's relation to the future of black identity. Only part of the ambiguity can be explained by reference to the uncertainty of how distant this future is. However, it is important to recognize that Sartre does not ask Jews to renounce their identity. Indeed, as we saw, his critiques of the Enlightenment position points him in a very different direction as his account of the authentic Jew shows. The position Sartre adopted in 'Black Orpheus' is thus anomalous.

Sixty years after Sartre's study was written it is easy to be amazed at the way he overlooks the complexity of the questions raised by anti-Semitism. Judged as an investigation of the phenomenon and as a possible basis for addressing it, *Anti-Semite and Jew* is flawed. Indeed, some critics have tried to show Sartre as unwittingly reflecting in his own ideas the anti-Semitism he wanted to combat. To be sure, by acknowledging his own responsibility, his own anti-Semitism and that of his fellow Frenchmen, Sartre shows all those who are not Jews that their fate cannot be separated from that of the Jews. In keeping with what he wrote about responsibility elsewhere, as we saw, Sartre acknowledges that our complicity with the anti-Semites had, because it leads straight to National Socialism, 'made hangmen of us all'. Sartre's essay is not to be understood as an academic study, but as a dramatic intervention relating to a pressing problem of the moment. It was one of the first of many occasions when he would show how his philosophy had the power not simply to illuminate reality, but to work towards changing it.

8

'THE EYES OF THE LEAST FAVOURED'

The skilled worker has always based his demands on the qual-
ifications necessary for his work. He is the true producer, the
sole source of all wealth: he transforms the raw material into
social goods. The idea of a general strike, so popular before
1914, grew out of this proud self-consciousness. In order to
bring down bourgeois society, the worker has only to fold his
arms [. . .] Since its rights flow from its merits, this aristocracy
is not far from considering itself the sole victim of capitalism.
[. . .] This humanism of labour is ambiguous: one will readily
admit that it goes a step beyond the humanism of wealth. And
yet it is only a stage; if one stops there, the multitude will
remain excluded from humanity. It is necessary, you say, to
merit being a man. That is fine as long as one can *acquire*
merit. But what are you going to do with those who do not
have the means for acquiring it?

The new proletariat cannot claim the least merit, since
everything has been brought into play to make it understand
that it hasn't any. Yet fatigue and misery overwhelm it: it must
die or obtain satisfaction. On what, then, will it base its
demands? Well, precisely on nothing. Or, if you prefer, on the

demands themselves. The need creates the right. With the appearance of the masses, an overturn of values took place; automation radicalized humanism. Let us not take the semi-skilled worker for a proud man conscious of his rights: he is 'a subhuman conscious of his subhumanity' who demands the right to be a man. The humanism of need is, consequently, the only one that has all humanity as its object: the elimination of merit blows up the last barrier which separated men. [. . .]

Today the two humanisms coexist and this coexistence muddles everything: if the former becomes set and establishes a position for itself, it becomes the enemy of the latter. The masses, on the other hand, are secretly contaminated by the ideology of the workers' élite. They have no shame before the bourgeois; for the best of them, no matter what he does, will never *merit* the privileges he enjoys; but the skilled workers belong to the proletariat [. . .] The apparent inequality of conditions stresses in his eyes the inequality of values; if the skilled worker derives his worth from his operation, the semi-skilled worker is worth nothing since he is, by definition, replaceable. In short, he is ashamed before those who ought to be his comrades in arms; [. . .] it was necessary to make the masses understand that they were offering all men the chance to look at man and society *in their truth*, that is to say, with the eyes of the least favoured. [. . .] The *masses* are not worthy; they can't even imagine what freedom is: but their simple existence introduces, like a splinter in the flesh, the radical demand for the human in an inhuman society.

Communists and Peace.

During the 1950s Sartre's philosophy underwent significant changes. To a large extent these were the result of the transformations that were taking place in world politics. When, towards the end of 1944, soon after the liberation of Paris, Simone de Beauvoir, Maurice Merleau-Ponty, Raymond Aron and other prominent French intellectuals of his generation joined forces with Sartre to establish the journal *Les Temps Modernes*, the global situation was serious and uncertain. For a while it was far from clear whether or not France would end up on the side of the Soviet bloc or the United States of America: France was in the middle and could have sided with either of these great powers that had contributed to its liberation from the Nazi occupation. From the first issue in October 1945 *Les Temps Modernes* promoted democracy and opposed 'revolution by law'. It also opposed the Indo-China War, which France was fighting to protect its south-east Asian colonies. Aron quit the journal in 1946, accusing it of left-wing bias. Certainly, as its political positions developed, this was the general direction in which it evolved. By 1948, editorials in *Les Temps Modernes* were attacking the United States for its 'racism and implicit fascism'. In 1949, they targeted the British Labour Party for its imperialism. However, during this period it was Merleau-Ponty, not Sartre, who was largely determining the political positions adopted by the magazine. Because the sympathies of the editorial board of *Les Temps Modernes* lay with the proletariat, they sought to reach some kind of understanding with the French Communist Party, but, so far as the Party was concerned, Sartre and de Beauvoir were both so famous that they were seen not merely as a distraction, but almost as rivals for the public's and the media's attention.

During the late 1940s Sartre looked for a neutral position in the conflict between the Soviet Union and the United States, but events ruled this out. Even though *Les Temps Modernes* came out against the Soviet forced-labour camps in

1950, the tendency was still to think of Russia as reflecting the future of humanity. Russia's declared intentions saved it in the eyes of many French intellectuals. McCarthyism in the United States, by contrast, had no such excuses. However, with the outbreak of the Korean War, Merleau-Ponty, and thus *Les Temps Modernes*, fell largely silent on the conflict between the two great powers and thus on the biggest political issue of the day. Meanwhile, Sartre had given up the idea of writing the promised sequel to *Being and Nothingness* that would be devoted to constructing an ethics. He had become increasingly suspicious of how ethics had been reduced to bourgeois morality. Ethics was ultimately vacuous, a way of propping up the status quo by telling the poor and oppressed that they would be stealing if they took back what was rightfully theirs. To prepare himself to address questions of political justice, Sartre was studying history, economics and Marxism. When towards the end of 1952 he finally took sides, it was to defend the Communist Party and to do so by writing in an idiom very different from any he had employed earlier. He now combined his passion for ideas with an attempt to take account of the facts as represented by statistics.

Sartre came to the defence of the Communist Party when it looked most vulnerable. Henri Martin, a Communist sailor, had been imprisoned in 1950 for distributing propaganda against the Indo-China War. After a demonstration against his imprisonment had turned violent, Jacques Duclos, president of the Communist group in the National Assembly, was himself imprisoned. A general strike was called but the response among the workers was poor, to the great satisfaction of the right-wing press. This was the occasion for Sartre to publish in *Les Temps Modernes* in July 1952 what was to become the first part of *Communists and Peace*. In full consciousness that he was unredeemably bourgeois, he aligned himself with the working class: 'You cannot fight the working class without becoming the enemy of men and of yourself.'[1] The basis of this view was Sartre's conviction that unless all are free, none are free: one therefore had to align oneself with the most oppressed members of society. Sartre argued further that one cannot be for the workers and against the Communist Party. The first essay of *Communists and Peace* is also important for Sartre's refusal to separate economics and politics. To the extent that one insists on their interconnection, one can highlight the contradiction between the way the bourgeois acknowledge the humanity of the workers and the way they treat them like animals. Sartre set out to expose that contradiction.

The second part of *Communists and Peace* appeared in *Les Temps Modernes* towards the end of 1952. Sartre insisted on drawing a distinction between the mass of workers as isolated individuals and their collective class existence as the proletariat. It is only as the proletariat that the workers are the subject of history; that is why Sartre thought that the Communist Party was indispensable. In his view, it is only through the Party that the working class takes on a unified existence. Without the Party, the workers remain in the situation capitalism made for them: their needs, as Marx already explained, put them in competition with each other for a share in the same limited resources, including jobs. So long as the workers thought of themselves as individuals, they were locked in a struggle for existence among themselves. Under those conditions the workers at best constitute a mass. Capitalism produces the workers, as the anti-Semite makes the Jew, but the bourgeois deny the existence of class. It is the Party that creates the working class in the sense of making it into a class of real unity, thereby preparing the people for the real struggle, which was against their employers, for better conditions and higher wages. For Sartre, the decisive feature of the proletariat is that it exists only so long as it acts.

Sartre became increasingly concerned with the way society operates such that the individual worker is isolated and rendered incapable of seeing how his or her interest lies in promoting the interest of the proletariat as a class. Already in the 1950s Sartre was beginning to identify the way modern democracies tend to use the secret ballot as indicative of that tendency. Public voting offers more room for buying votes and intimidation, but it also enables every voter to experience his or her solidarity with a class. With the secret ballot, the voter is readily addressed in terms of his or her individual interest and not according to the interests of society as a whole.[2] Later, in *Critique of Dialectical Reason*, Sartre would call 'serialization' this process whereby society is divided into so many isolated individuals, whose individuality is regarded on the model of atomic particles. Serial thinking thus highlights the distances that divide a society into its fragments. By identifying serialization not just as a way in which societies are organized, especially in modernity, but also as a form of thought, Sartre succeeded is refining his critique of what he had earlier, for example in *Anti-Semite and Jew*, opposed in analytic reason. Nevertheless, even though his observations of the crisis of the French Communist Party in the early 1950s enabled him to clarify how the class interest of the proletariat was rendered invisible, he was still in search of a way to reverse this tendency. This would in *Critique of Dialectical Reason* lead him to an account of dialectical reason that was firmly tied to action, but what makes *Communists and Peace* so important for understanding the development of Sartre's thought is watching how features of his philosophy already in place in *Being and Nothingness* were summoned to the task.

The third part of *Communists and Peace* appeared in 1954. It is the richest part and the one from which the above extract is drawn. However, as with the previous parts, Sartre's account is deeply immersed in events in France at the time, a fact that perhaps accounts for the way the whole volume, in spite of marking a decisive step in Sartre's itinerary, is largely ignored today. He not only offered a somewhat gloomy view of the state of the economic system in France at that time; he also exposed the violence, largely under the surface, that sustained the system. Sartre also gave a rather pessimistic account of the possibility of moving forward because of the lack of unity within the working class. He set out to show how the proletariat in 1900 were internally differentiated so that one might even talk of 'the dictatorship of the skilled élite'. The skilled worker can bring production to a halt indefinitely in a general strike but, in part because of this, puts himself above the unskilled workers. This creates a division within the working class that finds its basis in the different sets of values to which they adhere. Things were rendered ever more complicated by the advent of the semi-skilled worker who is a product of modern machines and the kind of organization such machines impose on those who operate them.

In an effort to clarify the situation Sartre introduced a distinction between three kinds of humanism, thereby establishing a framework that would be carried over into the *Critique of Dialectical Reason*. According to the first, the classical humanism of the bourgeois (which he here calls the humanism of wealth), the bourgeois recognize the workers as human. However, this of itself does not encourage the bourgeois to treat the workers any better. Indeed, fear that the workers will one day exact their just revenge provides a basis for treating them even more harshly. In this way this classical humanism forms the basis for a kind of class racism that is directed especially against the semi-skilled workers. Then there is, second, the humanism of labour, which Sartre regards as ambiguous, because it is blind to the conditions that determine the distribution of skills throughout society. The humanism of labour is not yet a humanism for all humanity. This takes place only with the advent of a third kind of humanism, the humanism of need. The humanism of need is not only directed towards ensuring that everyone has enough to survive, but also towards creating humanity. At its basis is the recognition that, because so much of humanity is leading a deprived life, the task before us is not to redistribute the wealth of society more evenly so that more people can share the lifestyle of the rich, which is a viewpoint most typical of those on the verge of being middle-class; rather the task is to invent for the first time what it means to be human, on the grounds that humanity cannot yet have been realized in such a divided world where the differentials of wealth and power are so enormous. It is from this perspective that violence can come to be seen as not a means to the end of a better or improved society, but as itself a form of positive humanism. Emancipatory violence is already humanism in action. These sentiments found their fullest expression in Sartre's famous preface to Fanon's *Wretched of the Earth*, written in 1961.

To address the gulf separating the skilled workers from the rest of the proletariat – with whom they are united by interest but from whom they are divided by their adherence to a humanism of labour that refuses the humanism of need – Sartre had recourse to the idea of shame. He had given a powerful description of shame in *Being and Nothingness*. The example is of someone who, while looking through a key-hole, hears footsteps down the corridor, and suspects he or she has been caught. From being the observer, the voyeur has become the observed; from occupying the subject position, he or she has been reduced to an object; or, in Sartre's own terminology, the for-itself has become in-itself. This description enables Sartre to recognize the power of the gaze in general. In his account of concrete relations with others, Sartre had highlighted the way that the gaze projects an identity on someone who is then trapped in it. We saw this idea in operation in our discussion of *Anti-Semite and Jew*: it is through the gaze that the anti-Semite makes the Jew. This structure had already been illustrated in *Being and Nothingness* with the example of the workers who are constituted as such by the gaze of the bourgeois. As shown in the above extract, in *Communists and Peace* Sartre modifies the fundamental structure of shame to account for the divisions in the working-class movement and to propose a different way forward. Whereas in *Being and Nothingness* he had dismissed the role of need in accounting for the self-identity of the workers as such and instead highlighted the gaze of the bourgeois, in *Communists and Peace* needs are clearly central. Furthermore, it is not the gaze of the bourgeois that deprives the semi-skilled workers of the initiative and reduces them to inaction, but the gaze of the skilled workers: 'he is ashamed before those who should be his comrades in arms'. Nevertheless, even though the shame the unskilled workers experience before the skilled workers paralyses and divides them, Sartre acknowledges the significance of the gaze of the unskilled and what it harbours. Sartre here enunciates a principle that had already surfaced at various places in other works but had never been central until this moment: the idea that the demands of the least favoured members of society express the truth of a society, not least because their interests are often in clear contradiction with the values espoused by that society itself.

To be sure, because Sartre at this time was still defending the place of the Communist Party, while not endorsing all its actions, he limited the power of the gaze of the least favoured in deference to the Party. Indeed, part of the motivation for the essay was to defend the Party against an attack by Claude Lefort (1923–), a former student of Merleau-Ponty. According to Sartre, Lefort was only able to speak about the workers from a distance. Only the Communist Party could speak in the name of the workers. In *Communists and Peace*, therefore, the gaze of the least favoured introduced an independent principle of judgement, which Sartre could only do once he had abandoned his faith in the Communist Party. After the Soviet invasion of Hungary in 1956 he could no longer underwrite the role he had previously given to the Party. That the Party in some sense creates the proletariat as a revolutionary group presupposes the existence of the Party but offers no adequate answer to the question of how it itself is formed, or what the source of its legitimacy is. Sartre began to suspect that under many circumstances the Communist Party was illegitimate. Indeed, the Party is only legitimate when it acts as the real representative of the proletariat, but this can often not be possible. He therefore abandoned the announced fourth and final part to *Communists and Peace*, and wrote *The Ghost of Stalin* instead, in which he offered a more dialectical account of the relation of the Communist Party to the proletariat. The Party had served a mediating role that was indispensable but it had solidified its structures in such a way as to compromise its usefulness.

Communists and Peace was very much about France, and

even at the time of writing it. Sartre knew that its analysis
could not be sustained in isolation. In the course of the text
he highlighted the fact that most blacks in French West Africa
had a standard of living inferior to the least favoured whites,
and he acknowledged that the prosperity of the advanced
countries was built on the misery of others. The least favoured
were outside Europe and the truth of European society was to
be found in its exploitation of the colonies. Sartre would
increasingly construe the disadvantaged not primarily as the
semi-skilled workers but as the colonized. He passed to a
global perspective in which decolonization loomed large, cul-
minating in his preface to Fanon's *The Wretched of the Earth*. It
is worth recalling therefore that Sartre's discussion of the gaze
in *Communists and Peace* follows a model that he had already
introduced in 1948 in 'Black Orpheus', where he described
the negritude poets as also reversing the gaze: instead of
whites defining blacks, whites in this poetry could experience
themselves as seen. By their gaze and by the poetry they wrote
primarily for a black audience, the negritude poets shamed
whites, signalling the advent of a new order whose first
expression would be the struggle for decolonization.

Sartre thus resorted increasingly to what underlay his commitment to the least favoured members of society, the
downtrodden: their gaze, which led him to experience his
shame. Sartre's shame as a member of the bourgeoisie had
paralysed him when it came to passing political judgements on
the Party. His initial way of expressing solidarity with the
workers was to defend the Party; he now rediscovered his
independent critical voice, but it was still at the service of the
disadvantaged. The masses, unlike the negritude poets, are
portrayed in *Communists and Peace* as almost mute, too
exhausted to speak for themselves, and thus needing the Party.

However, they too were given a more prominent role by Sartre following his disillusionment with the Party, and he embraced a version of what has come to be known as 'standpoint epistemology' that gave the oppressed more credit for having insight into the cause of their suffering.

9

'A FUTURE MORE OR LESS BLOCKED OFF'

For us man is characterized above all by his going beyond a situation, and by what he succeeds in making of what he has been made – even if he never recognizes himself in his objectification. This going beyond we find at the very root of the human – in *need*. [. . .] The most rudimentary behaviour must be determined both in relation to the real and present factors which condition it and in relation to a certain object, still to come, which it is trying to bring into being. This is what we call *the project*.

Starting with the project, we define a double simultaneous relationship. In relation to the given, the *praxis* is negativity; but what is always involved is the negation of a negation. In relation to the object aimed at, *praxis* is positivity, but what is always involved is the negation of a negation. In relation to the object aimed at, *praxis* is positivity, but this positivity opens onto the 'non-existent,' to what *has not yet* been. A flight and a leap ahead, at once a refusal and a realization, the project retains and unveils the surpassed reality which is refused by the very moment which surpassed it. [. . .] The material conditions of his existence circumscribe the field of his possibilities (his work is too hard, he is too tired to show any interest in union or political activity). Thus the field of possibles is the goal toward which the agent surpasses his objective situation. And this field in turn depends strictly on the social, historical reality. For example, in a society where everything is bought, the possibilities of culture are practically eliminated for the workers if food absorbs 50 per cent or more of their budget. The freedom of the bourgeois, on the contrary, consists in the possibility of his allotting an always increasing part of his income to a great variety of expenditures. Yet the field of possibles, however reduced it may be, always exists, and we must not think of it as a zone of indetermination, but rather as a strongly structured region which depends upon all of History and which includes its own contradictions. It is by transcending the given toward the field of possibles and by realizing one possibility from among all the others that the individual objectifies himself and contributes to making History. The project then takes on a reality which the agent himself may not know, one which, through the conflicts it manifests and engenders, influences the course of events. [. . .]

Every man is defined negatively by the sum total of possibles which are impossible for him; that is, by a future more or less blocked off. For the under-privileged classes, each cultural, technical, or material enrichment of society represents a diminution, an impoverishment; the future is almost entirely barred. Thus, both positively and negatively, the social possibles are lived as schematic determinations of the individual future. And the most individual possible is only the internalization and enrichment of a social possible.

Search for a Method.

In 1957 Sartre was approached by the editors of a Polish journal who were preparing a special issue on French culture.

They asked him to write a piece on the current state of existentialism. Sartre's response was an essay entitled 'Existentialism and Marxism' in which he had a great deal more to say about Marxism than existentialism, which reflected where his interests then lay. Towards the end of the same year a heavily revised version appeared in *Les Temps Modernes* under the title 'Questions de méthode'. He regarded it as so important that he reprinted it, with the addition of a new conclusion, in the *Critique of Dialectical Reason*. It is this version of the essay that was translated into English as *Search for a Method*.

Sartre's view at that time was that at any moment in history only one living philosophy expressed the general movement of society and that the philosophy of the current epoch was Marxism. He also believed that once everyone came to enjoy a modicum of genuine, concrete freedom, then a philosophy of freedom would replace Marxism, but that at the present juncture there was no way of conceptualizing the character of this freedom or the philosophy that would arise from it. According to this conception, existentialism was not the philosophy of freedom that belonged to the future but was, rather, entirely subordinate to Marxism. The task of existentialism was to rescue true Marxism from the Communists, who had entirely subverted it by reducing it to a form of idealism. Just as Sartre in his essay on intentionality had avoided idealism by finding the human being out there in the world among things, so he now rejected that form of Marxism that had reduced man to an idea: existentialism addressed human beings where they live – at work, at home and on the street. Existentialism, as a philosophy of the concrete, had now found its indispensable historical task, but on the condition that the concrete was now identified as 'history and dialectical action'.

Sartre's attempt to unite existentialism and Marxism has

not always been well understood because commentators have been inclined to focus on the superficial characteristics of both movements rather than their deep structures. Existentialism tends to be seen as promoting individual freedom, whereas Marxism is viewed as a materialist and deterministic philosophy. Sartre tried to disturb this opposition by citing a letter that Friedrich Engels wrote in January 1894.[1] In the letter Engels attacked a strict economic determinism, albeit while affirming the priority of economics for understanding history. The central sentence, to which Sartre returned on a number of occasions, reads: 'Men themselves make their history but in a given environment which conditions them.' Sartre used this statement to attack those Marxists who preached a form of economic determinism. He insisted that authentic Marxism maintains that under conditions of exploitation man is both a historical agent and a product of his product. The task he set himself was to think both ideas together. This called for a new understanding of dialectics and to prepare for that task he refined his account of the limitations of analytic reason.

Sartre had long recognized the difficulty of restoring what analysis had rent asunder, but recognition of that problem was a recurrent insight within twentieth-century phenomenology. What was new in *Search for a Method* was that he recognized more clearly than anyone the political consequences of the dominance of analytic reason. In keeping with his claim that at any one time there is never more than one living philosophy, Sartre acknowledged that analytic reason at one point had had an emancipatory force by virtue of its capacity to divide and dissolve: analysis empowered the French bourgeoisie to challenge the institutions of the *ancien régime*. Indeed, the French Revolution merely destroyed institutions that analytic reason had already dissolved. Analytic reason went on to articulate a liberalism, but in the process it became oppressive to the extent that it contributed to the 'atomization of the Proletariat'. In so far as liberalism is an ideology committed to individualism, it is unable to account for groups. It is thus resistant to a class analysis. In this way, analytic reason at a certain historical point shifts from being oriented to creating a new future and comes instead to perpetuate the status quo; at that point its tendency to see only separated individuals and exclude the possibility of seeing the various ways in which those individuals are bound together in society presents a serious obstacle to the overthrowing of the present system, given that, as we saw in the last chapter, recognition of class interest is a precondition for radical change.

Sartre's long-standing suspicion of analytic reason as the exclusive form of reason came into its own with his discovery of the dialectic. He had used the word 'dialectic' in earlier texts, but, like many people, seemed to be able to say little about it, beyond calling for a synthetic movement to breathe life into the rigid construction that is left as a residue of analysis. *Search for a Method* was Sartre's announcement that he now intended to rehabilitate the dialectic, and the main body of *Critique of Dialectical Reason* was the place where he sought to fulfil that promise.

In his effort to understand the dialectic in terms of history, Sartre starts with embracing concrete persons, in their materiality, that is to say, in their labour and their relations. He solicited Marx's help against those Marxists who confused concrete reality with an abstract determination, like György Lukács (1885–1971). Lukács was one of the main targets of Sartre's critical spirit, not because he was necessarily the worst of contemporary Marxist theoreticians, but, one suspects, because he had repeatedly attacked Sartrean existentialism.

One of Sartre's barbs against Lukács was the idea that he was no more capable than any other Marxist of understanding Heidegger. There was a great deal at stake in that claim because the *Critique of Dialectical Reason* is not only Sartre's most Marxist book but also his most Heideggerian. Or, more precisely, it shows a deeper understanding of *Being and Time* than he had shown previously, even though Heidegger's name is not mentioned as often as it was in his earlier works. The best indication of Sartre's new appreciation of Heidegger is the fact that he now returns to the attempt to bring together freedom and facticity, of for-itself and in-itself, and of project and situation, begun in *Being and Nothingness* but not successfully accomplished there. In the later work, the language of *Being and Nothingness*, with its talk of the project as a transcending or giving beyond a situation towards a future in action, is retained, but it is now combined with an account of the project expressed in Marxist terms, albeit following a model that owed more to Heidegger and Marx. The project mediates between two moments of objectivity: the given situation and a possible transformation. Sartre had always recognized that the given situation is never simply given and that we always transcend it simply by living it, but, although his phenomenological descriptions showed this, his reliance on analysis to present his ontology in terms of the dualism of for-itself and in-itself undercut the descriptions.

Sartre's insight was to take from Heidegger the recognition that the way that the projection of possibilities determines the situation is most readily apparent in work and action. He added on his own part that need and scarcity, both of which played only a marginal role at best in *Being and Nothingness*, underlie work and action. That is to say, the recognition of the ultimate significance of need transformed Sartre's philosophy by transferring attention to materiality, and this, as the above extract shows, was fully integrated into the idea of the project. The result is a dialectical account of action. Or, more precisely, an account of action that serves as a basis for understanding the dialectic in the conventional sense of a negation of the negation. Action, or, as he also calls it, praxis negates the given and, in so far is the given is defined by need, praxis is the negation of a negation. The negation of the negation towards a new positivity is always a determinate negation. Action thus unveils the limitations already circumscribed within a given situation, limitations that from the perspective of the future appear as contradictions within existence.

In 'Existentialism is a Humanism' Sartre accepted Francis Ponge's (1899–1988) formulation 'man is the future of man'. In *Search for a Method*, he had found a perspective from which to view societies in terms of the ways they blocked off or opened up the future for the classes that constitute that society. With this idea that closes the above extract, Sartre completes the shift from the individual perspective to a societal perspective.

Although his expressed aim in *Search for a Method* was to use existentialism to revitalize Marxism, what one sees in the above extract is Sartre using Marxism to fulfil existentialism's long-standing ambition to be a concrete philosophy. The language of *Being and Nothingness* is still present in the description of going beyond the given situation towards a future in action, but because this movement of transcendence is rooted in need, Sartre had to modify his account of the project. We have seen in previous chapters how, for Sartre, the project sets various possibilities conceived in any situation that determine how present reality appears. For example, it is in terms of the ambition to have a career as a doctor that certain features of one's society appear as obstacles and others as opportunities.

In the pages immediately after the extract above, Sartre developed an example that illustrates this. It is drawn from an essay by Claude Lanzmann (1925–) that had been published a few years earlier in *Les Temps Modernes*.[2] It illustrates the way society circumscribes a person's possibilities, including his fight against the limitations it imposes on him. The example concerns a black man who, while working as ground crew at an airport, is expressly forbidden from flying because of his race. Sartre raises the question of the various ways one might respond to this restriction, which was directed not against this particular black man personally but against his race. By stealing a plane and flying it solo across the English Channel, this rebel revolts by taking up a future that was forbidden to him. Sartre believed that this act of revolt already presses towards a different future for blacks. Indeed, resentment is already a surpassing that moves beyond the given situation. But it only gets so far. Sartre suggests that it would be wrong to see the rebel as breaking the mould imposed on him by society. The possibility of rebellion has in a sense been foreseen by the law and so can easily be contained. Even more significant is that this oppositional gesture is by an individual and that others do not join it. The contradiction of a society that discriminates between the races is both concealed and surmounted in his project.

Sartre's growing appreciation of the difficulties of changing society persuaded him to find some consolation and hope even in isolated gestures of rebellion. What is new in *Search for a Method* is that he is clearer than ever before about how the fact that one becomes aware of one's class through recognition of a possible future can itself serve the generation of class consciousness. Sartre is clear throughout the book of the cost of a lack of class consciousness. He rehearses Engels' example of how, during the 'war of the peasants' in the sixteenth century, some groups of peasants, separated from other groups in other parts of Germany, each made a separate peace. Their apparent victory was, from a broader perspective than was visible to them, a defeat for their whole class. However, through becoming conscious of itself a class could under certain conditions recognize itself in history. To the extent that it did so that class would become the agent of history for that period.

10

'MAN IS VIOLENT'

The 'discovery' we have made in the course of our dialectical investigation [. . .] has revealed, at different levels, the double character of human relations: apart from the determinations of sociality, as simple relations between real but abstract individuals, they are immediately reciprocal. And this reciprocity – mediated by the third party, and then by the group – must be the basic structure of the community. [. . .] And it is clear that the conditionings of antagonistic reciprocity are, as a whole, and *in the abstract*, based on the relation of the multiplicity of men to the field of action, that is, on scarcity. We have also seen that scarcity, as a mortal danger, produces everyone in a multiplicity as a mortal danger for the Other. The contingency of scarcity (that is to say, the fact that relations of immediate abundance between other practical organisms and other milieux are not inconceivable *a priori*) is reinteriorized in the contingency of human reality. A man is a practical organism living with a multiplicity of similar organisms in a field of scarcity. But this scarcity, as a negative force, defines, in commutativity, every man and partial multiplicity as realities which are both human and inhuman: for instance, in so far as anyone may consume a product of primary necessity *for me* (and for all the Others), he is dispensable: he threatens my life to precisely the extent that he is my own kind; he becomes inhuman, therefore, as human, and my species appears to me as an alien species.

[. . .] [T]he primary determination of morality is Manichaeism: the intelligible and threatening *praxis* of the Other is what must be destroyed in him. But this *praxis*, as a dialectical organization of means with a view to satisfying need, manifests itself as the free development of action in the Other. And it is clear that it is this freedom, as my freedom in the Other, which has to be destroyed if we are to escape the *danger of death*, which is the original relation between men through the mediation of matter. In other words, the interiorization of scarcity as a *mortal* relation between men is itself performed by a free, dialectical transcendence of material conditions and, in this very transcendence, freedom manifests itself as a practical organization of the field and as perceiving itself in the Other as other freedom, or as an anti-*praxis* and anti-value which has to be destroyed. At the most elementary level of the 'struggle for life', there is not blind instincts conflicting through men, but complex structures, transcendences of material conditions by a *praxis* which founds a morality and which seeks the destruction of the Other not as a simple *object* which is dangerous, but as freedom which is recognized and condemned to its very root.

It is precisely this that we have called *violence*, for the only conceivable violence is that of freedom against freedom through the mediation of inorganic matter. We have seen, in fact, that it can take on two aspects: free *praxis* may directly destroy the freedom of the Other, or place it in parentheses (mystification, stratagem) through the material instrument, or else it may act against necessity (the necessity of alien-ation), that is to say against freedom as the possibility of becoming Other (of relapsing into seriality), and this is Fraternity-Terror. Thus *violence* is *always* both a reciprocal recognition of freedom and a negation (either reciprocal or univocal) of this freedom through the intermediary of the iner-tia of exteriority. Man is violent – *throughout* History right up to the present day (until the elimination of scarcity, should this ever occur, and occur *in particular circumstances*) – to the anti-human (that is to say, to any other man) and to *his Brother* in so far as he has the permanent possibility of becoming anti-human himself. This violence, contrary to what is always claimed, envelops a practical self-knowledge because it is determined by its object, that is to say, as the freedom to annihilate freedom. It is called *terror* when it defines the bond of fraternity itself; it bears the name of *oppression* when it is used against one or more individuals, imposing an untranscendable statute on them as a function of scarcity.

Critique of Dialectical Reason.

The first volume of the *Critique of Dialectical Reason*, the only volume published during Sartre's lifetime, is almost eight hun-dred pages long, if one includes 'Search for a Method', the essay that preceded it in the French edition. Even so, readers can be forgiven for thinking that in the course of the book Sartre makes relatively little progress towards his stated goal of answering the question of whether Marxism possesses the resources for identifying the structures that must govern any future anthropology. Sartre, as always, offers some rich exam-ples of the structures he explores. His vivid descriptions of the way people standing in line at a bus stop relate to each other, and the way in which the hit parade that lists the top ten records perpetuates itself the following week because so many people make it their business to buy what everybody else is buying, both brilliantly illustrate what Sartre calls seriality, just as his account of the storming of the Bastille illustrates a fused group. These descriptions are as memorable as the examples of the waiter in the café or the man looking through the keyhole in *Being and Nothingness*, but the danger is always that one remembers the examples and not what they are supposed to illustrate.

Although one major problem of the book is that it stops far short of its stated goal of establishing a foundation for a dialectical rationality that would secure the possibility of historical knowledge, another problem is the fact that it is, uncharacteristically for Sartre, badly written. Simone de Beauvoir explains that Sartre wrote the book intensively, working long hours with the aid of stimulants, and without revising the text, as he normally did. The final extract in this book illustrates the difficulty of reading Sartre when one goes beyond the illustrations and finds him at his most abstract. The extract, which is taken from late in the *Critique of Dialectical Reason*, represents one of his attempts to summarize the fundamental perspective that arises from it. He does so in terms of the 'discovery' that he refers to at the beginning of the extract and which we explored in the previous chapter, which is that praxis is itself dialectical. In this chapter I shall explore the broader implications of this approach and I shall argue that, in spite of the flaws that I have mentioned, the *Critique* is a masterpiece, perhaps *the* great work of political philosophy of the twentieth century.

Sartre constructs his account of dialectical reason on the basis of the discovery that man is 'mediated' by things to the same extent that things are 'mediated' by man. He calls this 'dialectical circularity'. It bears a striking resemblance to Heidegger's so-called hermeneutic circle or 'circle of understanding', in so far as it is based on the same reciprocal relation of project and situation that was already operative in Heidegger's *Being and Time* and, as we saw, was borrowed by Sartre to establish the framework for the account of freedom in *Being and Nothingness*. However, what differentiates Sartre's position in the *Critique* from his earlier account, and Heidegger's account for that matter, is his strong focus on the material conditions as they impact on the project. Indeed, in what appears to be a remarkable turnabout, Sartre at one point in the *Critique* dismisses the idea, which he attributes to the Stoics, that 'man is free in all situations'. Of course, this idea of total freedom is usually understood to be more Sartrean than Stoic, but Sartre protests that his own views are the opposite of this: all men are slaves in so far as they inhabit a realm conditioned by scarcity. Indeed, he says explicitly that the slave is not free in his or her chains. However, one should not overestimate the extent to which Sartre has modified his position. As we saw, the political dimension of his account was always there and he in no way wants in the *Critique* to back away from the idea that freedom is a project that unifies the material circumstances into the practical field that in turn gives rise to that same project.

Sartre's contention is that contemporary Marxists focus almost exclusively on the extent to which individuals are determined by their material circumstances; individuals submit passively to the relations of production and other forces in which they find themselves and by which they are conditioned. He deplores the fact that these Marxist accounts passed straight away to a discussion of the concrete conditions, while neglecting the need to begin with an abstract account, as Marx himself had done. The result is that the Marxists deprive themselves of the resources of the dialectic. As a corrective to this approach, Sartre begins in the *Critique of Dialectical Reason*, as he also did in *Being and Nothingness*, with the abstract in order to proceed by stages to the concrete. To be sure, Sartre sees the task differently in both of these books. In *Being and Nothingness* his concern is, as we have seen, that if one begins with the concrete rather than the abstract, one lacks a vital radical tool with which to challenge existing societies, in the way that his notion of freedom challenges the lack of freedom in society as we know it. In the *Critique of Dialectical Reason* something similar is going on. Above all, he wants to show that if one takes existing society as given, one overlooks the history which creates that society, and in particular one overlooks the extent to which human beings make society by their activity and are not merely the product of society.

But there is another benefit of beginning with the abstract, specifically the abstract individual: it shows how one cannot construct an account of concrete society on the basis of such abstract units. They will undergo radical transformation as the account becomes more and more concrete. That is why only a dialectical presentation can do justice to the task of describing concrete society, because the very terms of the description must be produced by the account. Above all, society cannot be understood as the sum total of the individuals who constitute it. Society is a set of human relations and it would be better to understand the individual as constituted by those relations than vice versa. To this extent, the later Sartre, as is increasingly recognized by commentators, is much closer than is usually recognized to the theorists of the death of the subject, such as Claude Lévi-Strauss (1908–) and Michel

Foucault (1926–84), who argue that the idea of the subject that has dominated philosophy since René Descartes (1596–1650) has no basis in reality.

So if the above extract from Sartre's book appears abstract, it is in a sense supposed to be, because, although the book was never completed, it did become progressively more concrete. Some of Sartre's readers seem to treat the abstract discussion of human relations that one finds in the opening sections of the *Critique* as representing his own view, as if they were not to be corrected later as he proceeds towards the concrete. It is as if, for them, the famous example of the view from an upper-storey window of two workmen going about their business oblivious of each other because they are separated by a high wall somehow describes the truth of society. Worse still, because Sartre in this way takes as his starting point individuals who are completely isolated by institutions and by their social condition, they attribute to him the same social atomism that he considered to be the product of analytic rationality. In fact, he believed that it was the vocation of dialectical rationality to overcome this analytic rationality by exhibiting the concrete bonds that might seem to be entirely exterior, but which can be shown to be interior.

The governing assumption is that the theoretical problems will disappear when we arrive at the concrete and that even as one moves closer to a concrete account then things become clearer. For example, Sartre seeks here to overcome what he regarded as the false dichotomy between individualism and communitarianism. Nevertheless, he believes that individuals have a reality that collectives lack. But it is not the individual of analytic rationality, the isolated individual, that is real. So Sartre begins the *Critique* with the isolated individual in an

effort to show precisely the inadequacy of any such abstract
characterization. By studying reciprocal relations between a
pair of individuals and by showing how such a study means
always going beyond two people to what Sartre calls the third,
he tries to provide a more concrete account of inter-human
relations. In this way the abstract moment of the investigation
is indispensable, but inadequate. Indeed, its inadequacy is very
much to the point.

Sartre's account is unquestionably formal by his own admis-
sion and it needs to be. Of itself, therefore, this does not
constitute a criticism, although it does lead to some absurd
moments in the text. For example, as an illustration of a positive reciprocity, Sartre offers the example of a sports team.
The movements of each member of the team call forth a corresponding movement by the others, so that, when they
function as a unit, each supporting the others, one can legitimately talk of their acting together in a common praxis.
Nevertheless, Sartre qualifies this analysis in a hilarious footnote that reveals the level of abstraction at which his account
of the team was operating: 'In fact, in a football match, everything is complicated by the presence of the opposite team.'[1]
Even 250 pages later, he is still acknowledging that the
account he had developed up to that point of a class's internal
relations to itself at the level of class struggle was still so
abstract that he had not yet included the hostile action of the
enemy class or classes. This is the absurd side of Sartre's enter-
prise and an indication of why it was so difficult for him to
complete the book.

Sartre provides a better example of his method when he
takes up the case of a colonialist who believes himself insulted
by a Muslim servant and so beats him. It is not as an individual that the colonialist does this so much as because this is

what a colonialist does in such a situation. The other colonialists beat their servants and so when this colonialist gives his servant a beating, one cannot really say that he acts of his own initiative, but in fulfilments of the actions of others. Similarly the servant who allows himself to be beaten is responding differently from how he would if another member of his own class treated him in this way. He understands the beating to be addressed to him as a Muslim, as one of the colonized. Sartre does not deny that there are two real individuals going through this pantomime that is repeated again and again throughout the colonies, but he does deny that the event can be described adequately by focusing exclusively either on the individuals concerned or on the irrealizable identities of colonialist and colonized. As we saw in chapter four, according to the early Sartre the identity of being a waiter is irrealizable: one can never be reduced simply to being a waiter. Similarly here, one acts as others – colonialists, for example – act. It is the Other (the colonialists) in me who beats the Other (the colonized) in him. This complex relation is a mark of each individual's alienation. The later Sartre in this way enriches his earlier analysis of how group identities operate by adding a touch of Marxism. More precisely, the difference between early and late Sartre on this point is that whereas in *Being and Nothingness* each individual is involved in a direct battle for supremacy, in the *Critique* the antagonism is mediated both by a social identity that dictates certain patterns of action and by scarcity at the material level.

Within our history scarcity sets individuals against each other so that co-existence is impossible. Even before this is interiorized as a struggle to survive in which everyone is in principle a rival, the danger of annihilation that threatens oneself and others is something one finds in one's own activity. However, when scarcity is internalized, the people see each other as the principle of evil and thus as targets to be destroyed. It is this that enables Sartre to say that the first movement of ethics is the constitution of Manichaeism. Sartre used the term 'Manichaeism', which is the name of a Babylonian religion in which good and evil were recognized as independent principles, to describe the way in which, as a result of material shortages, the Other is constituted as threatening one's capacity to survive and thus as radically evil.

Nevertheless, in *Critique of Dialectical Reason* Sartre is not only attempting to challenge liberalism's atomic individualism, but also to offer an apparatus that can explain the brutality of the French Revolution and the Communist regime in Russia. In brief, Sartre argues that the 'fused group' that accomplished the Revolution by acting as one inevitably collapses into what he calls seriality, where what binds the individuals concerned are ties no tighter than those that unite the prospective passengers standing in line waiting for a bus. In a doomed attempt to prevent the fused group collapsing into seriality its members bind themselves together by taking an oath that is violently enforced. The result is that the fused group collapses into what Sartre calls 'fraternity-terror'. This shows how far he is from proposing a form of communitarianism. Society, at least society as we know it, is made up of individuals. That is to say, the individual as such is not a myth, only the abstract atomistic individual of bourgeois liberalism is.

It is tempting today to dismiss the *Critique of Dialectical Reason* as a book made irrelevant by the collapse of Communism and the resulting reduction of Marxism to a historical relic. However, these new circumstances open it to new approaches. On its publication, some Third World activists, like Frantz

Fanon, immediately saw its importance, although professional Marxists seemed more concerned to judge whether it met the prevailing standards of Marxist orthodoxy. By contrast, it can today be allowed to stand on its own as a strikingly original attempt to resolve long-standing philosophical problems that have not disappeared.

More precisely, Sartre succeeded in developing a philosophy that not only gave an account of the basis and operation of oppression, but also showed how adherence to an exaggerated individualism contributes to the persistence of that oppression, by inhibiting awareness of the solidarity that might allow the oppressed to join together to fight oppression. He also succeded in showing how the idea of the individual with which we tend to operate is based on an abstraction that leaves behind much that is fundamental to human existence. At the same time as he launched this attack on individualism, he refuted communitariarism by showing that in order to sustain themselves groups ultimately must have recourse to means that end by tearing them apart. In this way he succeeded in pointing the way beyond both individualism and communitarianism, the two poles which still tend to define most debates in political philosophy today. The great achievement of Sartre's mature philosophy and his enduring legacy is that he not only found a way to restore the concrete individual that, as he already argued in 'Intentionality', academic philosophy had lost sight of, but that he did so while at the same time allowing for genuine, if only fleeting, moments of solidarity. For this reason, the *Critique of Dialectical Reason* may well be a neglected masterpiece, a work of such magnitude that the history of twentieth-century thought will one day have to be entirely rewritten in order to acknowledge its significance. For all its flaws, it showed the need to break the official monopoly of analytic reason over all forms of thought and, more importantly, it indicated some ways in which the task of thinking dialectically might begin.

NOTES

3: 'Hell Is Other People'

1 Jean-Paul Sartre, *Being and Nothingness*, trans. Hazel Barnes, London: Methuen, 1957, p. 429.

4: 'He is Playing at Being a Waiter in a Café'

1 Cf. *The Imaginary*, trans. Jonathan Webber, London: Routledge, 2004, p. 191.

5: 'In War There Are No Innocent Victims'

1 Georg Wilhelm Friedrich Hegel, *Lectures on Natural Right and Political Science*, trans. Peter Wannenmann, Berkeley: University of California Press, 1995, p. 307.

2 Jules Romains, *Verdun*, trans. Gerard Hopkins, New York: Alfred A. Knopf, 1939, p. 443.

3 Jean-Paul Sartre, *War Diaries*, trans. Quintin Hoare, London: Verso, 1984, p. 16.

4 Jean-Paul Sartre, *Truth and Existence*, trans. Adrian van den Hoven, Chicago: University of Chicago Press, 1992, p. 46.

5 Jean-Paul Sartre, 'The Republic of Silence' in *The Republic of Silence*, ed. A. J. Liebling, New York: Harcourt, Brace, & Co., 1947, p. 498.

6: 'I Am Obliged to Want Others to Have Freedom'

1 François Jeanson, *Sartre and the Problem of Morality*, trans. Robert V. Stone, Bloomington: Indiana University Press, 1980, p. 22.

2 Jean-Paul Sartre, *Sartre by Himself*, trans. Richard Seaver, New York: Urizen Books, 1978, pp. 74–5.

3 Jean-Paul Sartre, *Notebooks for an Ethics*, trans. David Pellauer, Chicago: University of Chicago Press, 1992, p. 325.

7: 'The Authentic Jew Makes Himself a Jew'

1 Joseph de Maistre, *Considerations on France*, trans. Richard A. Lebrun, Montreal: McGill-Queen's University Press, 1974, p. 97.
2 Frantz Fanon, *Black Skin, White Masks*, trans. Charles Lam Markmann, New York: Grove Weidenfeld, 1967, p. 181.

8: 'The Eyes of the Least Favoured'

1 Jean-Paul Sartre, *Communists and Peace*, New York: George Braziller, 1968, p. 8.
2 Sartre's fullest account of the impact of the secret ballot on democracy came later and can be found in 'Elections: A Trap for Fools' in *Life/Situations*, trans. Paul Auster and Lydia Davis, New York: Pantheon Books, 1977, pp. 198–208.

9: 'A Future More or Less Blocked Off'

1 Sartre said that the letter was written to Karl Marx, even though at the time it was widely thought to have been written to Hans Starkenburg. However, it is now clear that although Stakenburg published it, the addressee was in fact W. Borgius.
2 Claude Lanzmann, 'L'homme de gauche', *Les Temps Modernes*, 10, 112–13, May 1955, pp. 1648–9. Lanzmann, who at that time belonged to Sartre's circle, later became renowned as the director of *Shoah*, a nine-and-a-half hour documentary on the Holocaust.

10: 'Man Is Violent'

1 Jean-Paul Sartre, *Critique of Dialectical Reason*, trans. Alan Sheridan-Smith, London: New Left Books, 1976, p. 473.

CHRONOLOGY

1905 Jean-Paul Sartre born in Paris on 21 June.

1906 Sartre's father dies.

1917 His mother remarries and the new family moves to La Rochelle, where Sartre is so unhappy that he temporarily loses the passion for reading and writing that he has enjoyed from an early age.

1920 Returns to Paris, where his love of writing is restored. His parents did not move back until 1922.

1924 Enters the prestigious Ecole Normale Supérieure. During his four years there, he attends only a few lectures, but the stimulation of his fellow-students, including Raymond Aron, George Canguilhem, Jean Hyppolite, Maurice Merleau-Ponty, and, a childhood friend Paul Nizan makes these years among the happiest of his life.

1927 Sartre and Nizan collaborate on a translation of Karl Jaspers' *General Psychopathology*.

1928 Fails the written examination. Nizan joins the Communist Party, but Sartre does not.

1929 Meets Simone de Beauvoir in July and they quickly became very close, working together for the examinations in which Sartre comes first and de Beauvoir second. In November, begins an eighteen-month stint in the military at St-Cyr.

1931 Accepts a position teaching philosophy at the *lycée* in Le Havre. Sartre and de Beauvoir consider marriage but reject the idea, regarding it as a bourgeois institution which limits freedom.

1933 In September he begins one year of study at the French Institute in Berlin. Although disgusted by the Fascists, living in Germany does not make him any more political.

1936 Takes up a teaching post at the *lycée* in Laon. His preliminary study of previous theories of the imagination, *Imagination*, is published, but the more original part will not be finished for another four years, when it appears as *The Imaginary (L'Imaginaire)*.

1937 Moves to a teaching position at a *lycée* in Paris and so is able to join Simone de Beauvoir who moved there the year before. Publishes 'The Wall', a short story.

1938 Publishes his first novel, *Nausea*.

1939 Publishes *Sketch for a Theory of the Emotions*. A collection of short stories, *The Wall*, meets with popular and critical acclaim. Mobilized into the army in September. A fascinating record of his reading and thinking during his military service is published posthumously as *War Diaries*.

1940 On his thirty-fifth birthday, Sartre is taken prisoner. In the camp, he lectures on Heidegger, writes a religious play and experiences a degree of comradeship with his fellow-prisoners that subsequently marks his philosophical view of the relation to others.

1941 Released from the camp on medical grounds by using the strabism in his right eye to pose as a civilian who has been declared unfit for medical service. He returns to teaching and also forms a Resistance group, 'Socialism and Liberty', that focuses on disseminating information. The level of danger to which Sartre exposes himself in his Resistance activities remains a matter of controversy to this day.

1943 Publishes a play, *The Flies*, and *Being and Nothingness*.

1944 The première of *No Exit* takes place in July. Sartre takes a leave of absence from his teaching post and never returns to it.

1945 Sartre spends the first part of the year in the United States as one of a number of French journalists invited to observe its war efforts. His often critical articles create some controversy. In October he delivers 'Existentialism Is a Humanism' to a packed audience in Paris. Publishes the first two volumes of the novel *Roads to Freedom*. A third volume appears in 1949 but the work is never completed.

1946 Again spends the early months of the year in the United States, in part to be with a woman called Dolores, one of a succession of women friends but one whom de Beauvoir found particularly threatening. The complete text of *Anti-Semite and Jew* appears.

1947 Publishes what would later be called *What is Literature?* in instalments in *Les Temps Modernes*.

1948 Publishes 'Black Orpheus', a preface to Leopold Senghor's anthology of negritude poetry. The Holy Office of the Catholic Church places all of Sartre's writings on the Index, its list of works Catholics are forbidden to read.

1952 Publishes *Saint Genet*, a study of the novelist that attempts to exemplify the process of existential psychoanalysis that Sartre has already determined to apply to Flaubert and that will occupy him off and on for the rest of his life.

1954 Visits Moscow for a month: his press interviews afterwards are largely uncritical. He goes there again in the following year after a two-month visit to China.

1956 Publishes 'Colonialism Is a System' in *Les Temps Modernes*. After the Soviet invasion of Hungary in October 1956, he denounces the Soviet Union and attacks the French Communist Party. However, relations with the latter were not entirely broken off because of their common opposition to France's war in Algeria.

1957 Publishes 'Existentialism and Marxism' in a Polish magazine.

1960 Publishes *Critique of Dialectical Reason*.

1961 Sartre's apartment is bombed in July because of his support of the Algerian struggle for liberation. A second bomb goes off the following year, but Sartre has already moved. Writes a powerful defence of revolutionary violence in his preface to Fanon's *The Wretched of the Earth*.

1963 Publishes *Words*, his autobiography of his childhood in which he explains how he had been seduced into the illusion of trying to live his life through the literary project.

1964 In October, tells the Swedish Academy that he wants his name withdrawn from the shortlist of candidates for the Noble Prize for Literature as he always refuses such prizes, but it is awarded to him anyway.

1965 Changes his mind about a planned visit to Cornell University, saying that he will not go to the United States while it is bombing North Vietnam.

1966 Takes part at Bertrand Russell's invitation in an international tribunal to address US war crimes in Vietnam. Elected executive president at the first meeting in London and in the following year presents its unanimous findings that the USA had engaged in terrorist bombings. The sessions are held in Stockholm after Britain and France deny the tribunal permission to meet in those countries.

1968 Offers his support to the student revolution in Paris. Later that year he not only attacks the Soviet invasion of Czechoslovakia, but also attends performances of his plays *The Flies* and *Dirty Hands* there. The plays are seen as encouraging resistance.

1970 After the editor of a Maoist newspaper, *La Cause du peuple*, is arrested, Sartre answers the call to take over as editor. By selling copies on the streets, he invites the police to arrest him, but as General de Gaulle famously says at the time: 'One does not arrest Voltaire.' He subsequently takes on the editorship of other radical journals in an attempt to protect them.

1971 Publishes the first two volumes of *The Idiot of the Family*, his existential study of Gustave Flaubert on which he has been working for almost twenty years. A third volume is published in 1972, but later in the same year the projected fourth volume (on *Madame Bovary*) is abandoned.

1973 The essay 'Elections, a Trap for Fools' argues against voting in a system where the voters are reduced to isolated individuals. Helps to launch a new daily newspaper, *Libération*, of which he is editor-in-chief.

1974 Forced to give up editorship of left-wing journals because of deteriorating health brought on by years of overwork and abuse of stimulants. He continues to engage in a variety of political debates.

1980 His conversations with Benny Lévy, *Hope Now*, are published. They remain controversial because some observers suspect Lévy of putting words into Sartre's mouth. Sartre dies on 15 April.

SUGGESTIONS FOR FURTHER READING

The best source for understanding Sartre's life is a trilogy of autobiographical volumes by his lifelong companion Simone de Beauvoir: *Memoirs of a Dutiful Daughter, The Prime of Life* and, most especially, *Force of Circumstances* (Penguin). These can be supplemented by two more conventional biographies: Annie Cohen-Solal's *Sartre* (Heinemann, 1987) and Ronald Hayman's *Sartre* (Simon & Schuster, 1987). There is also an incomplete but informative biography by John Gerassi with the wonderful title *Jean-Paul Sartre. Hated Conscience of His Century* (Chicago University Press, 1989). Sartre himself published an autobiographical text, *Words*, which is well worth reading in its own right, but it covers only his early years. Of more immediate use as an introduction to Sartre is *Sartre by Himself* (Urizen, 1978) which consists of a series of interviews and other materials that constitute the transcript of a film with the same title. However, the easiest and most reliable way to learn about Sartre's life as it relates to his literary production is through Kenneth A. Thompson's year-by-year and sometimes month-by-month account in *Sartre. Life and Works* (Facts on File Publications, 1984). This volume is also a useful reference work for biblio-graphical information, although on nothing like the scale of the first volume of Michel Contat and Michel Rybalka's *The Writings of Jean-Paul Sartre* (Northwestern University

Press, 1974). A new edition of this work, indispensable to scholars, is in preparation.

The best introduction to Sartre's thought is Ronald Aronson's *Jean-Paul Sartre: Philosophy in the World* (Verso, 1980). Unfortunately it is out of print, like many of the best books on Sartre. Bernard-Henri Lévy's engaging but self-indulgent tome, *Sartre: The Philosopher of the Twentieth Century* (Polity, 2003), is more readily available. The case for Sartre's continuing philosophical relevance was set out clearly by Christina Howells in the Conclusion to a useful collection of essays that she edited, *The Cambridge Companion to Sartre* (Cambridge University Press, 1992). Also useful in this regard is Nik Farrell Fox's *The New Sartre* (Continuum, 2003).

For background and further help reading Sartre's brief essay 'Intentionality', one might turn to Peter Caws' *Sartre* (Routledge, 1979). The best book on Sartre's literary works is Rhiannon Goldthorpe's *Sartre: Literature and Theory*, but unfortunately it does not serve all readers, as the quotations are given only in French. Sartre's own comments on *No Exit*, as well as his other plays, can be found in *Sartre on Theater*, edited by Michel Contat and Michel Rybalka (Random House, 1976).

For anyone interested in political issues a good entry point to *Being and Nothingness*, as well as to *Anti-Semite and Jew*, is Thomas Martin's *Oppression and the Human Condition: An Introduction to Sartrean Existentialism* (Rowman & Littlefield, 2002). On 'Existentialism Is a Humanism', and indeed all of Sartre's social philosophy, there is Thomas Flynn's *Sartre's Marxist Existentialism* (University of Chicago Press, 1984). The best introduction to *Critique of Dialectical Reason* is Pietro Chiodi's *Sartre and Marxism* (Harvester Press, 1976); I also recommend *Sartre's Political Theory* by William McBride (Indiana University Press, 1991). The political philosophy should not be studied without reference to the specific political causes promoted: however courageous and praiseworthy some of the political positions he adopted were, these were interspersed with misjudgements that must be viewed as indefensible. The best-informed survey of Sartre's politics was written by Ian Birchall under the title *Sartre Against Stalinism* (Berghahn Books, 2004).

One need look no further than Frantz Fanon's *Black Skin, White Masks* (Grove Press, 1967) and *The Wretched of the Earth* (Grove Press, 1968) to understand why Sartre has been regarded as such a valuable resource for discussions of race and colonialism, assuring him a strong audience in the Third World. However, in spite of his long relationship with Simone de Beauvoir, his track record on feminist issues is a great deal less impressive, although his philosophy still has useful resources: see *Feminist Interpretations of Jean-Paul Sartre*, edited by Julien S. Murphy (Pennsylvania State University Press, 1999).

Michel-Antoine Burnier's *Choice of Action* (Random House, 1968) is an invaluable study of both the context in which *Les Temps Modernes* was founded and the background of Sartre's political debate with Merleau-Ponty. The documents of that debate in its philosophical as well as its political dimension are presented together with an impressive array of secondary literature in Jon Stewart's collection *The Debate Between Sartre and Merleau-Ponty* (Northwestern University Press, 1998).

William McBride published in eight volumes a selection of some of the best essays on Sartre in English under the title *Sartre and Existentialism* (Garland, 1997). For current work on

Sartre, one can do no better than look at *Sartre Studies International*, which is published by Berghahn Journals in association with the UK and North American Sartre Societies.

INDEX